Susan Niner Janes was born in New York City and now lives in London with her husband and family. She has a degree in design from Cornell University, and has worked on and contributed to craft publications on both sides of the Atlantic.

Decorative Papercrafts

WORKSTATION

WORKSTATION is a new concept comprising all the elements you need to begin papercrafts.

Within the first 48 pages are a range of techniques and projects made using the tools and equipment supplied with the book. Additional pages of templates and patterns are provided at the back.

SUSAN NINER JANES

A DESIGN EYE BOOK

First published in 1995 by Design Eye Ltd.
The Corn Exchange, Market Square,
Bishops Stortford HERTS CM23 3XF

ISBN 1 872700 36 5

The Design Eye Team

Michael Tout
Lee Robinson
Aline Serra Littlejohn
Sally Symes
Joanne Coles

With thanks to our contributors
Keith Watson, Pamela Hopkinson and Compton Marbling.
Bowls on pages 38 and 39 by Judy Balchin.
Photography by Paul Forrester.
Illustrations by Madeleine David (pages 6, 8 and 9)
and Simon Byerley.

Manufactured in China.

ACKNOWLEDGEMENTS

To Leah, Daniel and Michael for their patience and encouragement,
and in memory of my grandmother Martha, who got me started in crafts.

Contents

Introduction

Paper is a versatile and exciting craft material. You can fold it, curl it, cut it, crumple it or mould it. Paper can be flat or 3–dimensional, smooth or rough, plain or patterned. It can masquerade as fabric or ceramics, or – exquisitely – be itself, paper. No other craft medium can match it for variety of appearance and texture.

Paper is readily available and inexpensive, making it ideal for creative experimentation. It is easy to work with, and so is perfect for beginners.

Because paper is so much a part of our everyday lives, we tend to take it for granted. So, starting now, make an effort to 'raise your paper–consciousness', and become aware of paper's potential for creative projects. When you come across paper packaging material or a container you can recycle, think about possible end uses – and squirrel your find away.

The suitability of paper as a craft material was recognised early on. Use of marbled papers can be traced back to the 12th century. Oriental cultures have a tradition of folded and cut papercrafts. When industrialisation brought down the cost of paper – and scissors – in the 18th century, papercrafts flourished in both Europe and America.

This book is a hands–on crash course in papercraft. Its aim is to acquaint and inspire you with the astonishing breadth of paper's creative potential and to provide you with a satisfying introduction resulting in attractive and useful projects.

The first section deals with methods of decorating paper – including the currently popular craft of stamping and the elegant art of marbling. The second part introduces many ways to create with paper. Skills featured include papercutting, origami, and papier mâché.

Instructions are given for techniques, as well as for specific projects. To get you off to a good start, this book comes equipped with some of the supplies and materials you will need.

May your venture into papercrafts be a fascinating and pleasurable experience.

Working with Paper

Understanding the properties of paper will help you achieve papercrafting success. This chapter shows how to handle and select paper, and introduces basic equipment and techniques.

The paper bends more easily in one direction

GRAIN

Grain is important when constructing with paper. Machine-made papers have a grain - an inbuilt directional preference. Grain affects the ease with which paper or card can be folded. A fold made with the grain will be crisp and sharp; folding against the grain produces an uneven, rough edge.

To test for grain, flex (do not fold) a sheet of paper, then turn the paper at right angles and repeat. The paper bends (and tears) more easily in one direction. When making up projects - fold with the grain whenever possible. If you fold card against the grain, lightly score it first to achieve a smooth edge.

STORAGE

Paper can be stored flat or rolled. Ideally, paper should be stored flat, laid out horizontally - but few of us have the space. One solution is to make a portfolio out of two sheets of card (see below), and keep your papers in it.

Paper can also be rolled up and stored in a cardboard or plastic tube. Roll paper with the grain, or unsightly marks may result.

MAKING A PORTFOLIO

1. Tape two large, thick pieces of card together along one long edge.
2. Tape the hinge on the inside, to protect the stored papers from the adhesive.
3. Cut a slit near the centre top of each side, thread ribbon through the slot and tie it to close the portfolio.

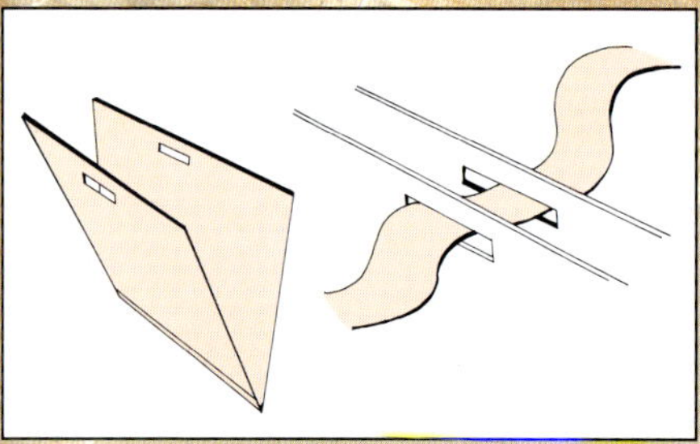

PAPER CHOICE

Choose papers to suit their function, judging them by appearance, weight, and 'hand' - the paper's feel and texture. Art supply shops are the main sources of purchased paper. Specialist shops sell 'art papers' which may be handmade, of high quality and unique appearance.

Here is a brief list of some of the papers particularly useful to the papercrafter:

1. ***Cartridge paper***
   A good all-round craft paper, inexpensive and easy to work with.

2. ***Cereal boxes***
   A handy source of lightweight card. Perfect for making pattern templates.

3. ***Corrugated card***
   Ridged packing material. Strong and flexible, adds surface interest.

4. ***Crêpe paper***
   Stretchy, fabric-like craft material with a pronounced grain.

5. ***Tracing paper***
   Useful for tracing and as a protective non-stick surface.

6. ***Gummed paper***
   Vibrant colours. Good for folk art cuttings (snip, lick, then stick).

7. ***Handmade paper***
   Has no grain and comes in unusual textures and effects.

8. ***Mounting board***
   Thick and sturdy card, suitable for making boxes.

9. ***Origami paper***
   Square, brightly-coloured on the face, white on the back. Sold in packs.

10. ***Paper twist***
    Twisted paper rope which can be spread out to reveal a strip of flat crinkled ribbon.

11. ***Polyboard***
    Made of polystyrene foam sandwiched between thin card. For making strong lightweight models.

12. ***Tissue paper***
    Translucent, fragile sheets come in a good range of colours.

Equipment

Papercraft requires just a few basic cutting and measuring tools, some of which you probably already own.

Cutting Tools

DECORATIVE EDGERS

Specially for papercraft, scissors with wavy, zigzag or scalloped blades. Fun to experiment with!

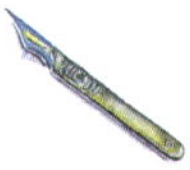

DESIGNER'S SCALPEL

For precise cutting of paper and thin card. Scalpels are also used to score card, cut partially through it to facilitate bending. Always cut against a metal straightedge, and on scrap card or a self-healing cutting mat.

SCISSORS

Small, sharp pointy scissors, such as embroidery scissors give you best control for intricate work. Use bigger scissors for rough cutting jobs.

SELF-HEALING CUTTING MAT

Protects the worktop, non-slip surface holds the card or paper as you cut.

Measuring Tools

RULERS

Metal rulers are required both for measuring and as straightedges, to cut against. Ideally, you should have several sizes: 6in (15cm) for small jobs, 12in (30cm) and 24 in (60cm) are useful sizes.

SET SQUARES AND PROTRACTOR

Essential for drawing and cutting accurate angles.

COMPASSES AND FLEXIBLE CURVE

These tools enable you to draw accurate circles, scallops and curves.

PENCILS AND KNEADABLE PUTTY RUBBER

Keep two pencils in your kit, so one is always sharpened. A kneadable rubber erases cleanly.

ADHESIVES

DOUBLE-SIDED STICKY TAPE

Sticky on both sides, with a peel-off backing. Convenient for sticking bows onto giftwrap.

MASKING TAPE

For temporary positioning of paper and card, and to ensure papers do not shift on the worksurface.

PVA (POLYVINYL ACETATE) ADHESIVE

Standard white craft glue. Dries clear and glossy, makes a strong bond. Use diluted, as a binder in papier mâché, and as a protective coating.

RUBBER SOLUTION

Dries quickly. Use for either temporary or permanent positioning. Good for bonding large areas of paper to card.

SPRAY ADHESIVE

Excellent for smooth bonding of large areas of paper to card. Use only in well-ventilated room on protected surface.

STICKY TAPE

Unsightly on most projects. use only for giftwrapping!

BONDING PAPER TO CARD

In papercraft, particularly when box-making, you may find yourself with a piece of decorated paper which is neither durable nor rigid enough to construct the desired project with. The solution? Bond paper to a base of sturdier card. There are several ways to do this:

Note: use a 'guardsheet' of clean paper to protect the decorated paper as you smooth it down.

- Use a glue stick for small projects. Coat the wrong side of paper in even, overlapping strokes. Starting at a lower corner, smooth the paper onto the card with the flat of your hand, working diagonally upwards.
- Use spray adhesive for larger areas. Spray the adhesive onto the card. Smooth paper onto the card. Roll up the paper and unfurl it as you go.

LAMINATING

Fusible web is an iron-on adhesive which can be purchased by the metre in fabric shops. Iron the web onto the wrong side of the decorated paper, then peel off the backing and iron the paper onto the card, starting at one lower corner and working upwards.

STAMPING

Any object that can carry – and deposit – pigment can be used for printing on paper. It is fun to experiment with printing with found objects, such as corks and leaves, but it is even more satisfying to create your own original printed designs with stamps. Stamps can easily be made using craft foam or sponge-cloth shapes stuck to card.

PLANNING YOUR DESIGN

Decide upon a design motif - a simple shape, such as a stylized leaf or a diamond, can be very effective. Good sources of pictorial inspiration include giftwrap, greetings cards and textiles - these have all been designed by professionals, so be guided by their expertise. Plan your design first on graph paper.

PATTERN REPEATS AND REGISTRATION

To make an all-over design, it is necessary to draw faint pencil guidelines on your paper so that your stamp can be positioned in a regular formation called the pattern repeat. Simple grid repeats, such as a side-by-side block pattern or off-setting the printing block for a less static half-drop repeat can be very effective.

The term 'registration' refers to the proper alignment of printed shapes. Mark registration guides on the top surface of the stamp, to help with positioning. For example, pen a little line on the top of the stamp so that it lines up with the centre of the stamped image. Repeat for all sides of the stamp. Sometimes the irregularity and imperfection of hand printing adds to its appeal. Anybody can buy a sheet of manufactured giftwrap!

No need to stick to straight edges. Let designs emphasize stamped motifs, like these fold-up notes and photo frame.

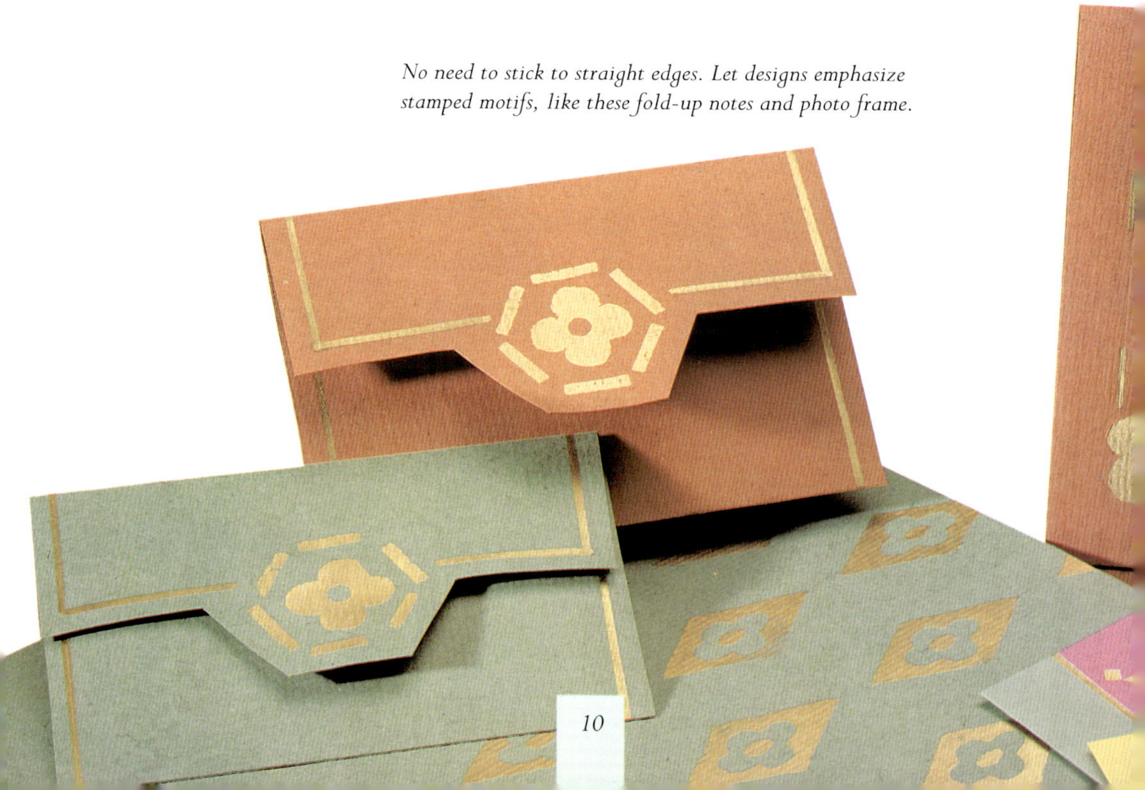

Making Rubber Stamps

YOU WILL NEED:

Supermarket sponge cloth 'wipe' or thin craft foam • Card from cardboard carton • Scissors • Designer's scalpel • Tracing paper • Pencil • PVA adhesive • Sponge roller (available from toyshops), or kitchen • sponge, or lino-printing roller • Designer's gouache, rubber stamp ink or a stamp pad (if stamp size permits) • Shallow dish or ice cream tub to hold ink

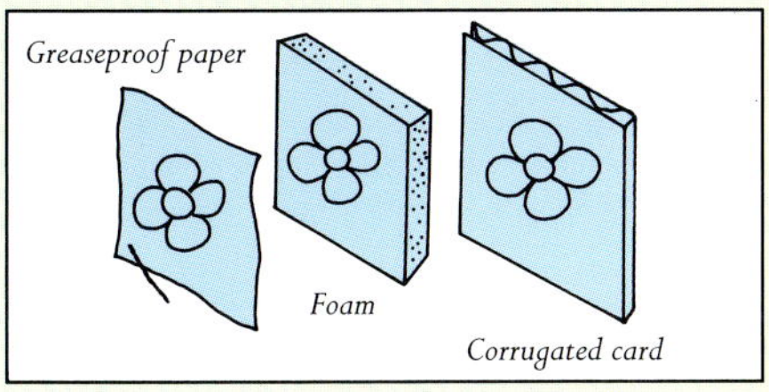

TO MAKE UP:

1. Trace off our pattern shapes from the back of the book, or design your own. Transfer outlines onto sponge cloth. Trace motif outline onto a small piece of card.

2. Using scissors and scalpel, cut shapes out of sponge cloth and card.

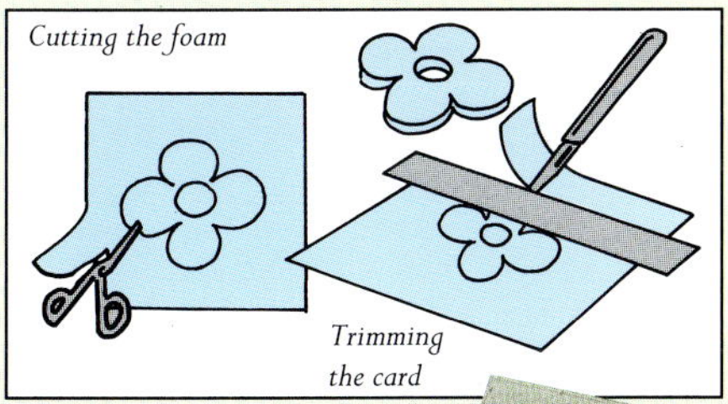

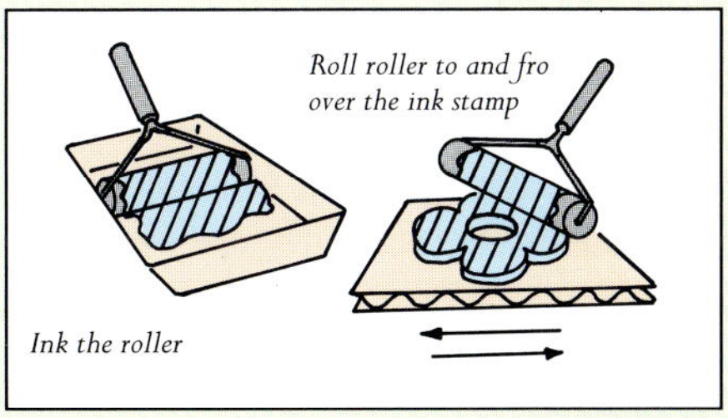

3. Glue the sponge cloth to the card backing. Thin designer's gouache with water to a creamy consistency. Spread the paint or stamping ink onto the bottom of an ice cream tub or shallow dish. Roll the roller over the stamp, coating it evenly. Alternatively, press stamp onto a purchased stamp pad.

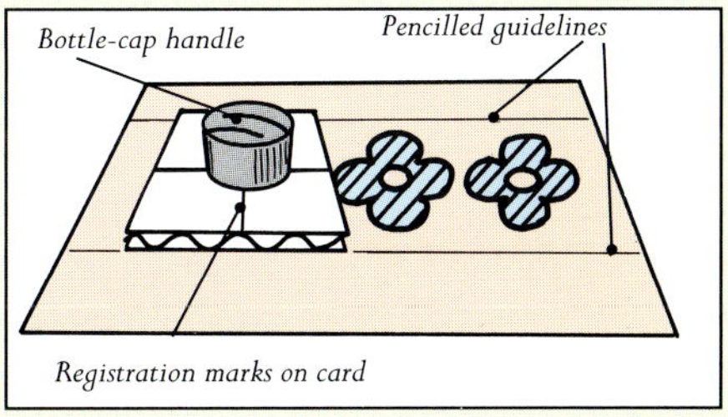

4. To print, stamp the paper surface firmly, holding the stamp straight on; then lift it cleanly, to avoid smudges.

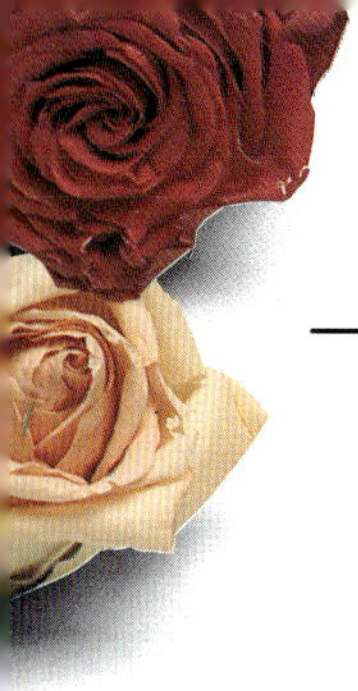

STENCILLING

A form of negative printing, Stencilling has been in use for hundreds of years as a simple decorative printing method. Instead of making an impression, as in stamping, a stencilled design consists of a cut-out area to which colour is applied.

Currently quite popular for home decorating, a large selection of ready-cut stencils and stencil books are on the market. Making your own stencils, however, is more creatively satisfying and is easily accomplished with a designer's scalpel and either a piece of acetate or lightweight card.

For ***Stencilling*** *you will need:*
Cutting mat or scrap card • Paints: designer's gouache, or acrylics • Palette • Applicators: stencil brush, sponge, old toothbrush • Masking tape • Paper to print on • Scrap paper

DESIGNING, CUTTING AND STENCILLING

Plan your design on paper, keeping the cut-out areas small. A basic shape is best for initial experiments. If using acetate, lay it on top of your design, tape in place, then cut out the design. If using card, trace the design onto the card, tape the card to the cutting surface, then cut out.

Temporarily fix the stencil to paper with masking tape. Mix up the paint, then apply paint to the cut-out area using one of the methods described below.

Carefully remove the stencil. Make sure the wrong side of the stencil is clean before using it again. If repositioning the stencil close by, wait until the paint is dry.

STENCILLING METHODS

SPONGE STENCILLING

An easy way to add texture to your designs. For each colour use a small natural sponge or cut a piece from a synthetic foam sponge. Make-up sponges are good for fine effects. Create a dimensional effect by concentrating the paint around stencil edges.

STENCIL BRUSH

Mix paint fairly thickly, dip in the brush, then dab off excess on scrap paper. Working with an upright brush that is nearly dry, dab on paint with an up-and-down motion. The dryness of the brush prevents paint from running under stencil edges.

TOOTHBRUSH STENCILLING

For an airbrush-like effect, dip an old toothbrush into paint that has been thinned, but is not runny. Dip bristle ends in paint, shake off excess then flick paint onto stencil, using your thumb to direct the spray.

REGISTRATION

For accurate positioning of stencils, draw (erasable) pencil guidelines on your paper that coincide with marked points on the stencil.

ROSE GARDEN PARTYWARE

YOU WILL NEED:

For stencils, thin card or acetate • Pastel pink paper • Mounting card • Designer's scalpel • Cutting mat • Metal straightedge • Scissors Cosmetics sponge • Paints: designer's gouache or acrylics • Light green satin ribbon, 1/4in (6mm) wide: 2 3/4yd (2.5m) for basket, 1 1/2 yd (1.2m) for each tray • Masking tape • Clear sticky tape • Glue stick • PVA adhesive • Greaseproof paper • Pencil • Ballpoint pen.

TO MAKE UP:

1. Trace off stencil motifs from the back of the book. You need four different motifs: 1 rose stencil, leaves for trays/napkin rings, leaf/stem for basket, leaf/stem for placemat.

2. Stencil material should be slightly larger all round than motif. Trace stencil outlines onto stencil material.

3. Carefully cut out stencils, discarding centre cut-outs.

4. Enlarge tray, basket, napkin ring and placemat patterns (see back of book) onto greaseproof paper. Reinforce stencil placement guidelines with sticky tape.

5. Bond pink paper to card using a glue stick. Cut pieces roughly the size of trays, basket and napkin ring. Cut a piece of pink paper roughly placemat size.

6. Place greaseproof paper patterns onto the pink card or paper, hold in place with masking tape. Trace over pattern outlines with a ballpoint pen, pressing firmly. The patterns will be 'engraved' on the card, to aid stencil positioning and cutting out of projects. Fix stencils in place with snippets of masking tape.

7. Mix up paint. Three colours are required: rose pink, mid-green and darker green.

8. Cut cosmetics sponge into fingers. Stencil leaves first. Hold sponge upright, dip in paint and blot on scrap paper till nearly dry. Dab into stencil.

9. Remove stencil, lifting it up cleanly like a hinge. Make sure the underside of the stencil is clean before using again.

10. Stencil roses when leaves are dry. On placemat, stencil alternate positions, then do motifs in between.

11. Make up the partyware following the instructions in the back of the book.

Paste & Combing

The paste-and-comb decorating technique was a favourite of bookbinders of long ago, who used it for their cover papers. The method is similar to fingerpainting and is just as much fun.

The paper surface is coated with coloured starch paste, which is then scraped away with a cardboard comb or a stylus, revealing the underlying paper. Patterns formed with this technique have a startling dimensional quality.

Paste papers curl up as they dry. You can flatten a dried paper by laying a board on top and weighting it with books. The best solution is to bond the paste paper to another surface (see page 9).

For ***Paste & Combing*** *you will need:*

Cornflour • Water-soluble pigment (gouache, acrylics) • Measuring cup and spoon • Saucepan • Mixing bowls • Card for making combs • Paintbrush, about 2in (5cm) wide • Artist's paintbrushes • Stylus • Cartridge paper for painting on • Old newspapers

MAKING PASTE PAINT

1. Blend two tablespoons of cornflour with the same amount of cold water in a saucepan.
2. Gradually pour in $\frac{1}{2}$pt (250ml) of boiling water, then stir constantly until the whole mixture comes to the boil and thickens. The mixture should have a creamy, gravy-like consistency.
3. Add colouring when the paste has cooled. Stir the pigment well, until the paste is lump-free.

MAKING PATTERNS

1. Lay a piece of cartridge paper on a sheet of old newspaper.
2. With a wide paintbrush, drizzle a line of paste along one edge.

3. Brush the paste on evenly, covering the whole piece of paper.
4. There are several methods of pattern-making. Work fast, the paint dries quickly. Dry the completed design on a fresh sheet of newspaper.

COMBING

Make a comb by cutting notches in a piece of card (also try the tines of a fork). Drag the comb across the wet starch, making zigzag or spiral patterns. By twisting a straight-edged piece of card, 'butterflies' can be made. Or, just use a stylus to draw a design.

STIPPLING

Apply the paste with brush, then stipple all over with a sponge, dabbing it up and down. Or apply paste, then texturize it with another type of brush.

Tip: Paper for paste painting must be fairly thick, or it will buckle when the paste is applied. Test a sample first.

Table-Top Accessories

YOU WILL NEED:
Decorated paper • Additional mounting card • Fusible web • An iron • Paper twist, for corner bows • PVA adhesive • Straightedge • Holepunch • Wavy-cut decorative edgers • Greaseproof paper • Pencil.

TO MAKE UP:
1. Make up the paste papers in two contrasting colours.
2. When papers are dry, iron a different-coloured sheet onto either side of a piece of mounting card using fusible web.
3. Enlarge the basket, snapshot frame and tray patterns (see back of book) to the appropriate sizes.
4. Transfer the pattern markings onto mounted paper.

TRAYS AND BASKET
1. Cut out and make up trays and basket following instructions in the back of the book.
2. Instead of cutting corner slits, punch holes at corners and tie on paper twist bows. If you prefer leave the handle off entirely.

SNAPSHOT FRAME
1. Make up following the instructions in the back of the book.
2. To finish, trim frame with wavy decorative edgers, just inside the pattern outline.

Fold & Dye

One-off patterned papers that resemble tie-dyed fabrics can be created by pleating absorbent paper and dipping it into water-soluble dye. The technique comes from Japan, so for authenticity's sake, why not seek out oriental rice- or mulberry paper, available from specialist paper suppliers? Other suitable papers are thin, soft and porous, such as tissue paper or newsprint. Kitchen roll is a convenient choice for your first attempts.

For ***The Fold & Dye Paper****, you will need:*
• Soft, absorbent paper • Water-soluble dye (food colouring, artist's dyes, or India ink) • Fairy cake tin or deep palette • Small bowl of water • Old newspapers • Clean scrap paper • Iron.

FOLDING

Prepare the paper by accordion-pleating it lengthwise. The thinner the paper, the more pleats can be formed. Next, accordion-fold the pleated strip into squares, rectangles or triangles (either equilateral or right-angled triangles are possible). Crease the paper sharply. When finished, the paper will be folded into a compact parcel.

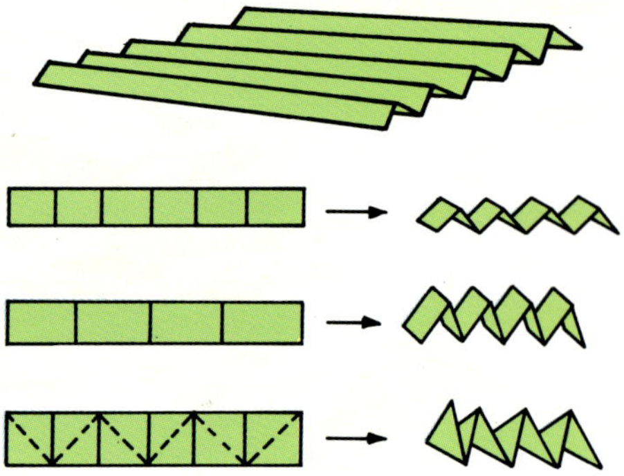

DIPPING

Protect the work area with old newspaper. Hold the parcel, compressing the area to be dyed. You can dip either a corner or a side of the parcel. The longer the dip, the greater the colour absorption. Dye colours can be overlapped. For a soft-edged, blurry effect, moisten the parcel in water before dyeing. Your fingers can be used to distribute the dye.

DRYING

Now for the tricky bit - opening out the paper. Do this gingerly and take your time; the saturated paper tears easily. When dyeing is complete, carefully unfold the parcel, revealing the original pleated strip. Blot the strip between two pieces of clean scrap paper.

Next, unfold the paper methodically and spread it out flat to dry on newspaper. When the paper is bone-dry, give it a press with a warm, dry iron. Cover the paper with a clean sheet of paper as you iron. The creases are an integral part of the design and cannot be ironed out completely.

The completed paper is quite delicate, and you may wish to strengthen it by bonding it to another sheet of paper or card (see page 9).

Hippy Dippy Gift Boxes

YOU WILL NEED:
Sheets of fold-and-dye tissue • Mounting card • Fusible web • An iron • Designer's scalpel • Pencil • Metal straight edge • Scissors • PVA adhesive • Paper twist • Greaseproof paper

For beads:
Cartridge paper • Narrow drinking straws, for winding • Varnish • Brush, for coating beads.

TO MAKE UP:
Make up boxes following the instructions in the back of the book.

FINISHING
1. *Make paper cylinder beads (see Paper Beads, page 30) in colours to match the box.*
2. *Tie a paper twist bow on each box. Snip each bow end in two, thread beads onto each strand, as shown. Knot end of each strand to secure beads. Snip into paper twist below knot, to form fringe.*

CHAPTER
• SEVEN •

MARBLING

The process of marbling, as we know it, originated in 15th century Persia or the Ottoman Empire. Prized for its unique appearance, the possession of marbled paper was often confined to a privileged few; the secrets of its manufacture cloaked in mystery.

By the 16th century, the craft had reached Europe, where marbled papers were in general use for bookbinding and decorative accessories, such as covered boxes.

Exactly how is marbling accomplished? To make marbled papers, paints are floated on a bath of water. The paints are arranged in a pattern, which is transferred onto the paper.

To ***Marble*** *you will need:*
A shallow tray • Marbling inks supplied with your Workstation • Stylus, such as a knitting needle • Thick cartridge paper, to fit comfortably into tray • Tap water • Strips of old newspaper, cut about (8cm) wide by tray width • More old newspaper (uncut).

1. Protect your worksurface and surrounding floor with old newspaper.
2. Wash out the tray and fill it up with tap water. Let the water settle, then skim the surface with a newspaper strip to remove dust particles.
3. When the water surface is still, shake the ink and add one or two droplets of each ink you wish to use.
4. Dip the stylus into the bath and swirl the colours to create a pattern.
5. Waiting only long enough for the surface of the bath to settle, gently lay a sheet of paper on top of the design. Gradually ease the paper down onto the water until it lies flat, taking care not to form an air pocket. After 2-3 seconds gently lift it from the tray and set it on several sheets of old newspaper to dry.
6. A second print can be taken from the tray - the colours will be less intense.
7. Clean up, skim the bath surface with a newspaper strip, removing all inks ready for the next design.

MARBLING TIPS

• Choose a light-coloured marbling tray - so you can see what you are doing!

• Most weights of paper can be marbled, but thicker paper curls up less. Don't forget that curled papers can be laminated onto card.

• Always use non-glossy paper for marbling. The inks will not adhere to a slick surface.

• Red, yellow and blue marbling inks are supplied with your Workstation - try mixing your own colours from these. Create marbling colours to suit end use.

• Keep a marbling diary, recording details of successful patterns and how you achieved them. Include reference swatches!

MARBLED DESK SET

The handsome desktop accessories over the page are made entirely from paper, and are inspired by traditional leather or bookcloth–trimmed marbled desk sets.

For the ***Marbled Desk Set*** *you will need:*
Sheets of marbled paper • Plain coloured paper to co-ordinate with marbling • Mounting card • Designer's scalpel • Metal ruler • Glue stick

BLOTTER

This is a conveniently smaller size than large traditional blotters, it takes an A4 sheet of paper - convenient in a small office or study area.

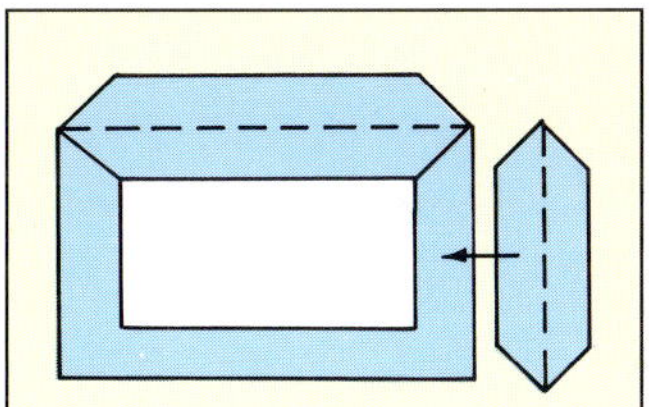

Apply strips to base

YOU WILL NEED IN ADDITION:
Medium weight card for base • Lightweight card for corners

TO MAKE UP:

1. *Cut the base measuring 9 1/2 in x 12 1/2 in (24cm x 32.5cm).*
2. *Cut corner tabs from two 3 1/4in (8cm) squares cut diagonally in half.*
3. *Base: from marbled paper cut two strips measuring 2 1/2 in x 12 1/2 in (6cm x 32.5cm) and two strips measuring 2 1/2 in x 9 1/2 in (6cm x 24cm). Mark the lengthwise centre on the wrong side of each.* *(Continued overleaf).*

(Blotter continued)

4. *Draw 1 1/4in (3cm) margins around the blotter base. Glue on the strips, folding each in half lengthwise to encase the blotter edges.*
5. *Corner tabs: cut plain paper to cover each corner tab, allowing a 3/8in (1cm) margin along the diagonal and 3/4in (2cm) margins along the straight sides.*
6. *Apply glue to a paper triangle. Place card triangle on top. Fold over diagonal margin.*
7. *Trim off excess paper. Repeat to make all four corners.*
8. *Glue the corners onto the blotter, slip an A4 sheet of thin card or blotting paper under the corner tabs.*

DESKTOP ORGANISER

This handy organiser will really help to keep your desk tidy! It is a variation on the basic tray pattern from the back of the book.

YOU WILL NEED IN ADDITION:

1 1/2yd (1.4m) ribbon 1/4in (6mm) wide • Holepunch • Felt-tip pen in matching colour

TO MAKE UP:

1. *Cut a piece of card slightly larger than the basic Tray Pattern from the back of the book.*
2. *Bond marbled paper to both sides of the card using a glue stick.*
3. *Cut out and score the pattern as instructed.*
4. *Cut four corner tabs from coloured paper. Fold up sides of tray then glue each corner tab in place.*
5. *Cover a piece of card with plain coloured paper. Cut out one long and one short tray divider. Punch corner holes in each divider.*

Marbled papers lend themselves to classic projects, like this desk set.

6. Slot divider together at centre intersection and set it into the tray.
7. To fasten divider to tray: pass a 15in (35cm) length of ribbon through each punched hole, thread ribbon through corresponding slits on tray side, tie into bows.

MINI TRUG

YOU WILL NEED IN ADDITION:
As for the Desktop Organiser but only 24in (60cm) ribbon

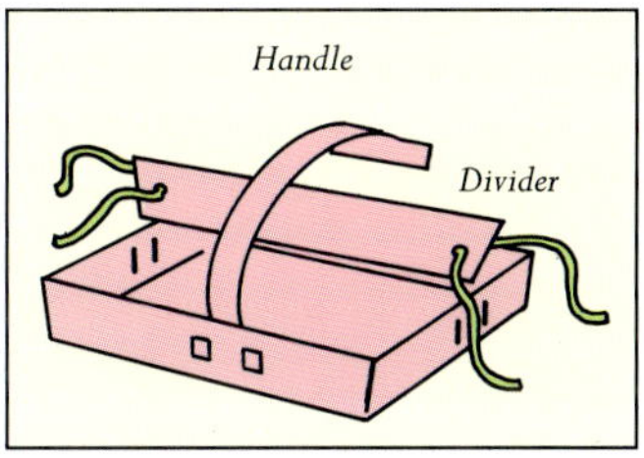

TO MAKE UP:

1. Enlarge mini trug and handle patterns from the back of the book.
2. Cover card on both sides with marbled paper.
3. Transfer pattern to card, cut out with scalpel. Score and cut slits as marked on pattern.
4. Cut the divider out of card covered on both sides with plain paper. Punch corner holes as indicated on pattern.
5. Insert divider, tying each side in place with a length of ribbon.
6. Insert handle tabs in side slits.

MINI NOTE PORTFOLIO

A smart folder to store A6 sheets of memo paper.

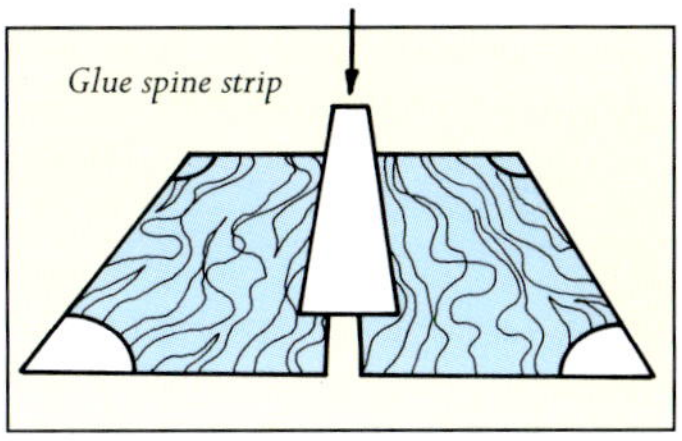

YOU WILL NEED IN ADDITION:
28in (70cm) ribbon 1/4in (6mm) wide • Compasses • Stapler

1. Cover a piece of card on both sides with marbled paper.
2. Cut out two pieces each measuring 4 1/2 in x 6 1/4in (11cm x 15.5cm).
3. Corner tabs: cut two, each is one-quarter of a 1in (2.5cm) radius circle.
4. Draw a 1/4in (1.5cm) margin along one long side of each piece of card. Glue a spine strip of plain paper to join both pieces of card. Glue corner tabs in place.
5. Staple ribbon close to centre of open edge of folder. Glue on paper to conceal staples. Tie ribbon in a bow.

PENCILS

To cover pencils, simply glue on strips of marbled paper. Do not sharpen until the glue is dry!

Cut Paper

Several deft cuts with a designer's scalpel – and pokes of an awl or nail – can transform a humble piece of paper into an attractive piece of patterned cutwork, with surface interest.

A cutwork pattern can consist of slits, flaps, perforations and cut-outs. Flaps can be folded to create dimensional interest. Think of a flap as an incomplete cut-out - a portion of it remains attached to the paper. If your design contains many flaps and cut-out areas, consider backing it with contrasting-coloured paper that will peep through the holes.

Cut-and-pierced designs look breathtaking when illuminated from behind. The Victorians were partial to cutwork lampshades; and Mexican folk artists have traditionally made cut-and-pierced tin lanterns, using much the same method. Use translucent paper behind back-lit cutwork.

Star And Heart Ornaments

For the ***Star and Heart Ornaments*** *you will need:*
Thin metallic card • Tissue paper • Designer's scalpel • PVA adhesive • Holepunch • Narrow ribbon • Decorative paper edgers.

1. Enlarge pattern from back of book, trace onto metallic card.
2. Cut out and edge the designs.
3. Cut a piece of tissue paper 1/4 in (6mm) wider all round than ornament's centre opening. Glue in place on wrong side.
4. On right side of ornament, glue on central metallic motif.
5. Punch out a few holes from metallic card. Glue punched dots around central star on heart ornament.
6. Cut several punched dots in half, then glue the 'half moons'onto star ornament as shown.
7. Thread a ribbon hanging loop through each ornament top.

Circular Papercuts

Most of us have made paper snowflakes as children. To make more sophisticated designs in the round:

• Start with a square piece of paper, fold it into sixths.

• With compasses, place point on apex and draw an arc close to the edge. Cut along the drawn line. Use decorative edgers to trim circle after it has been opened out.

Mexican Tin Style Hexagon Box

YOU WILL NEED:
Thin metallic card • Sturdy coloured card, for box • Designer's scalpel • Straight edge • Awl or nail • Decorative pinking edgers • PVA adhesive • Glue stick • Greaseproof paper • Ballpoint pen.

TO MAKE UP:

1. *Make up the hexagon box base and lid from the coloured card, following the instructions at the back of the book.*

2. *Trace off the pieces for the cut and pierced panels from the templates in the back of book.*

3. *Trace decorative panel designs onto right side of metallic card by pressing firmly along design lines with a ballpoint pen. For box, you need 6 side panels. For lid, you need, 6 side strips, 6 top panels and one lid cap.*

4. *Cut and pierce the box panels as in the photograph, then pink the panel edges.*

5. *Glue panels in place.*

CHAPTER • NINE •

Party Paperchains

Paperchains are traditional Christmas decorations, and hand-in-hand paper-doll chains are a standard nursery craft. Paper buntings and garlands are a useful way to decorate large areas quickly – that's why they are frequently used for parties and civic events. It's fun to come up with a fresh slant on a familiar idea. Paper chains have lots of design potential. Why not experiment with 3D effects (such as twisting or curling), unusual textures, or untraditional motifs?

PAPER CHOICE

Lightweight paper is ideal for chains. Gummed paper and origami paper are good for colourful details.

CUTTING TOOLS

Use short, sharp scissors. Embroidery scissors, or curved cuticle scissors, are excellent for intricate work. Single-fold or flat designs can be cut out using a designer's scalpel on a cutting mat.

CUTTING TIPS

To cut curves, instead of advancing the scissors, hold scissors stationary and feed the paper into the blades. If you must do intricate cutting with long scissors, cut with the part of the blades closest to the crosspoint. This will give you the most control.

3-D Flower Garland

1. Trace off pattern templates from the back of the book. Each flower has three pieces: leaves/backing, flower and centre. Reverse the leaves/backing template for alternate flowers.

2. Draw veins on the leaves, glue on the flower, then cut out.

3. Cut a slit in each flower centre, then glue into a cup shape.

4. For each flower centre, draw around a coin, then glue paper circles in place.

5. Cut slits as marked. Link flowers side-to-side by inserting tabs through slots and gluing down on underside.

Party Bunting

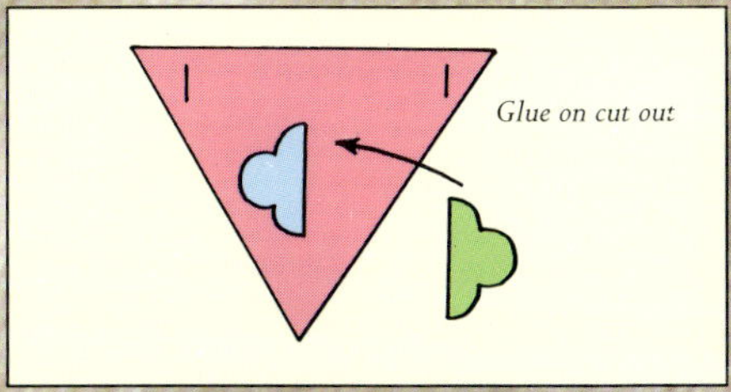

1. Trace off the triangular flags and motifs from the back of the book.
2. Cut out and stick down motifs.
3. Cut slits in flags. Join flags with standard paper chain links.

Lantern Chain

1. Trace off lantern pattern from the back of the book, cut out each lantern.
2. Each lantern is backed with a 2½in x 4 in (6x10.5cm) piece of contrasting coloured paper. Glue long edges of lantern to backing, aligning edges. Then glue the underlap.
3. Insert paper-strip handle through side slits.
4. Suspend lanterns from a conventional paper chain, as shown.

Zig-Zag Chain

[illegible] Each link of the chain is a strip of paper measuring [illegible].5x14cm. Fold each strip into quarters, as shown. Link up as shown in the diagram.

Paper Weaving

Flat strips of paper can be woven in much the same way as textile yarns. Either two sets of individual strips can be interwoven, or a single set of strips can be woven through a slit base card.

The simplest pattern to produce is an under-over basket weave, which creates a check pattern if the warp (vertically woven) and weft (horizontally woven) strips are of different colours. More complicated designs can be made by varying the weaving sequence. For example, a twill weave can be produced by weaving *under two, over one*. A book on weaving will give further ideas.

To add interest to woven paper projects try using papers with unusual textures (such as metallic or handmade papers), patterned papers, or strips that have been decoratively edged. If using the slit-base method, the slits can be cut wavy, slanted, or zigzag. You can also vary the width of the strips.

Woven Heart Baskets

YOU WILL NEED:
Two colours of thin paper • Narrow strip of paper for bow • Glue stick • Pencil • Designer's scalpel • Straightedge • Decorative edgers.

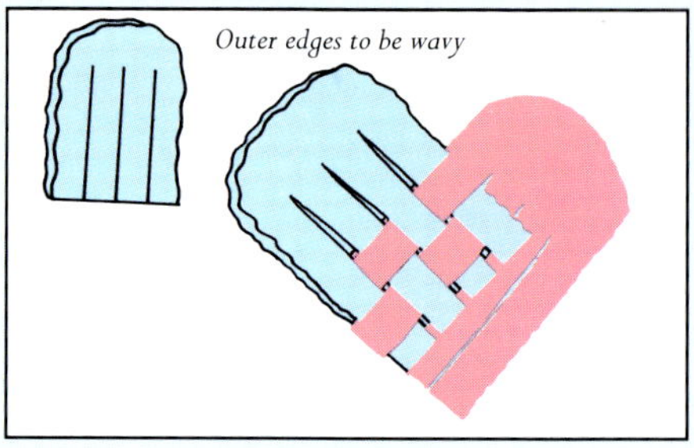

TO MAKE UP:

1. Glue coloured paper back-to-back.

2. Enlarge basket and handle patterns (see back of book) to large and small sizes. Transfer markings onto paper.

3. For each basket, cut out one basket handle and two basket bases. Cut out with decorative edgers, except for handle tabs.

4. Interweave basket bases according to diagram. (Each base piece should be turned to a different-coloured side.)

5. When weaving is complete, cut slits in each side of basket top and insert handle tabs.

6. Glue on paper bow.

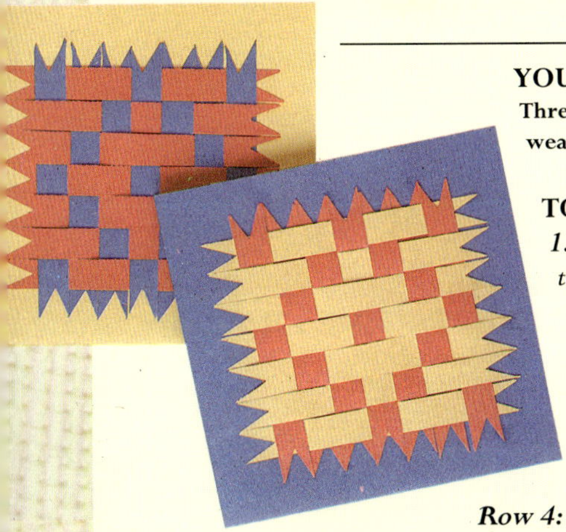

Woven Cards

YOU WILL NEED:

Three colours of cartridge paper (one for card, two for weaving) • Scalpel • Straightedge • PVA adhesive

TO MAKE UP:

1. *Weaving strips: cut seven double-pointed strips in two contrasting colours.*

2. *Align colour A strips vertically; glue top points to card front (strips centred).*

3. *Weave colour B strips horizontally:*

Row 1: *over 1, under 2, over 1, under 2, over 1.*

Row 2: *under 2, over 1, under 1, over 1, under 2.*

Row 3: *under 1, over 1, under 3, over 1, under 1.*

Row 4: *over 1, under 2, over 1, under 2, over 1.*

Rows 5 - 7: *work rows 3 to 1 in reverse order.*

4. *When finished, glue all free strip points to card.*

Woven Hexagon Basket

YOU WILL NEED:

Mounting card • Paper to cover card, such as kraft paper • Paper twist or crêpe paper • Designer's scalpel • Straightedge • Awl or nail • PVA adhesive • Glue stick.

TO MAKE UP:

1. *Enlarge the hexagon basket base and handle patterns from the back of the book. Copy the slits and dots on the hexagon basket base master pattern, but not the underlaps.*

2. *Bond paper to card with a glue stick.*

3. *Transfer pattern markings onto wrong side of covered card.*

4. *Cut out basket, including slits, scoring at base. Pierce holes at dots.*

5. *To make weaving strips, untwist the paper twist and cut it into 1 1/2in (4cm) wide strips. Alternatively, cut crêpe paper strips.*

6. *To assemble basket, fold basket sides up, then weave strips under and over the slits (one 'double under' is required at basket back to maintain pattern).*

7. *Join weaving strips by overlapping ends and gluing. Scrunch strips down.*

8. *Continue weaving in rounds until basket is complete. Tuck strip end to wrong side, glue down.*

9. *For corner bows, cut six 16in (40cm) long strips of 1in (2.5cm) wide twist or crêpe paper. Spiral a long strip around handle.*

10. *Join handle to base at either side of basket, by threading a 16in (40cm) strip through corresponding holes in handle and base, tie into bow.*

11. *Tie bows at remaining basket corners. Tie a bow at top of basket handle.*

QUILLING

Quilling, also called paper filigree or scrollwork, is the craft of rolling strips of paper into spirals and arranging them into decorative patterns that resemble the elaborate curlicues of ornamental ironwork. The craft was immensely popular during Victorian times, when a typical project might have been a hexagon box similar to the one here.

PAPER CHOICE AND CUTTING

Pre-cut strips of quilling paper are supplied with this Workstation. Cutting your own strips broadens the range of available papers. The paper should be flexible enough to be rolled, but firm enough to retain its shape, thin cartridge is ideal.

Uniform strip width is essential for a level design surface. Cut the strips on a protected worksurface, using a scalpel against a metal straightedge. Traditionally, the preferred width for quilling strips is 1/8in (3mm). Strip length varies according to the coil produced, but it rarely exceeds 12in (30cm).

HOW TO QUILL

1. Insert strip end into tool slot. Wind it round tightly once or twice.
2. Twirl tool to coil paper. Keep paper edges aligned, tension even.
3. For an open coil (ends not glued), release strip by giving tool a slight twist in opposite direction. Slide coil off tool.
4. To make a tight coil, glue strip down before removing tool. For a loose coil, release strip, let it spring open slightly, then glue end. Pinch into shapes shown on chart.
5. The completed coil may be mounted onto a surface using high-tack, white craft glue applied sparingly with a cocktail stick. Tweezers assist you in positioning the glued coils.

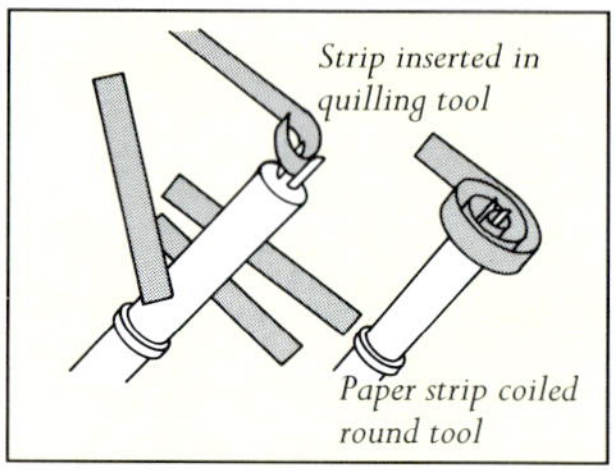

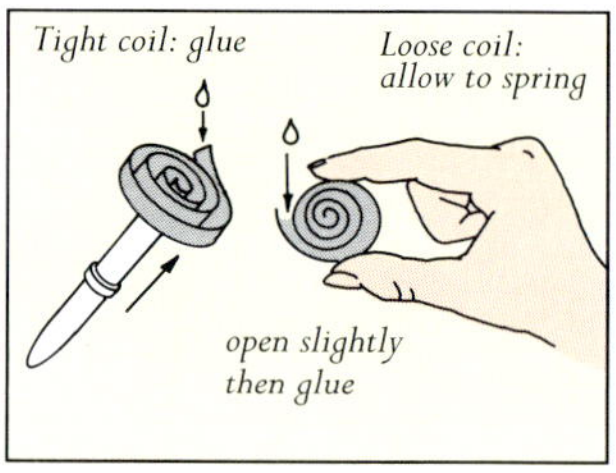

QUILLING SHAPES

There are two types of quilled coils, closed and open ended. Begin by mastering the closed shapes.

CLOSED COILS (strip end glued)

Tight coil

Glue end before removing coil from tool.

Loose coil

Remove coil from tool. Let it spring open slightly; glue end.

Eye

Pinch a loose coil at opposite sides.

Square or Diamond

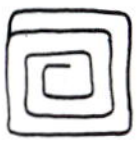

Make an eye, then pinch two more equidistant corners to form a square. For a diamond, make a square, turn it 'on point' then squash it down.

Star Coil

Make a diamond, then pinch corners firmly, creasing at centre of each side.

OPEN COILS (no gluing):

Loose open coil

Make a loose coil (do not wind end portion of strip). Let coil spring free.

Heart

Fold strip in half; coil each end towards centre.

V-Scroll

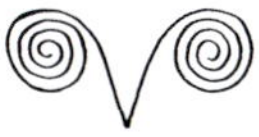

Same as heart, only strip ends are coiled outwards.

Scroll

Coil one end of strip towards centre, remove tool, then coil other end towards centre.

S-Shape

Coil strip slightly past halfway. Remove tool. Turn. strip around, then coil opposite side in same way.

Quilled Hexagon Box

YOU WILL NEED

Black card for box base • White card for box lid • Black and white cartridge paper for quilling strips • Quilling tool supplied with your Workstation • Designer's scalpel • Metal ruler • Pencil • PVA adhesive • Toothpicks

TO MAKE UP:

1. Cut out and score box pieces following the pattern at the back of the book.

2. It is easiest to glue the quilled shapes to flat base and lid before assembling the box. Use the photo as a placement guide.

3. Lightly pencil placement guidelines on each facet of the box and lid - mark centre of each box facet, and corner placement on base.

4. Make up the required quilled shapes. Apply glue to underside of each with a toothpick.

5. Box lid: place an eye in each corner, a diamond centre bottom of each facet. Centre medallion consists of centre coil surrounded by four scrolls. Each lid bottom panel has four adjacent S-scrolls.

6. Box base: glue an inverted heart scroll in each corner, and a star coil between these at either side. Centre medallion consists of a closed coil surrounded by four scrolls. At either side, glue a heart coil, then glue V-scrolls at top and bottom of medallion.

7. Assemble box lid and base.

Paper Jewellery

If you have mastered quilling, then making paper beads is simple, because the beads are rolled in the same manner as quilled coils. The difference lies in the shape of the paper strip. The basic paper bead pattern is an elongated triangle. Subtle variations in the degree of taper create the different bead silhouettes.

Paper beads are quick, easy and inexpensive to make, so you can afford to go over the top and come up with exuberant, riotously colourful designs. A variety of decorating methods can be used, including felt-tip pens, dimensional fabric paints, and the application of paper cut-outs. When finished with a coat of varnish, the beads are surprisingly durable. Why not make some in ethnic-inspired patterns, strung on silky macramé cord? Cartridge paper is a good material if you intend to decorate the bead afterwards. Patterned papers can be used to interesting effect, bearing in mind that the thinner the paper, the longer the strip required. Experiment and have fun!

Pages of glossy upmarket magazines are traditionally used for paper beads and provide an excellent opportunity for recycling. Paper quality is important - use monthly magazines which are printed on heavier paper rather than flimsy weeklies.

Patterned beads look best interspersed with plain-coloured, cylindrical spacer beads.

Lots of other attractive possibilities exist for paper jewellery - but in most cases, don't expect your jewellery to last. Make paper jewellery for the moment, and enjoy it for what it is. Paper jewellery is often just right for fancy dress or theatrical productions. You can make crêpe paper soft beads or, a woven friendship chain.

FOR STRINGING

Thread and clasps are supplied with your Workstation. You could also use silky macramé cord, leather thong, or narrow ribbons.

FOR DECORATIONS

Coloured felt-tips, dimensional fabric paints or scraps of coloured paper.

Bead	Pattern shape	Strip length	Width
 Cylinder		8in (20cm)	1/4in (6mm)
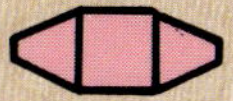 Rugby		16in (40cm)	1in (2.5cm) tapering to 1/4in (6mm)
 Barrel		16in (40cm)	1in (2.5cm) tapering to 1/2in (1.5cm)
 Chunky barrel	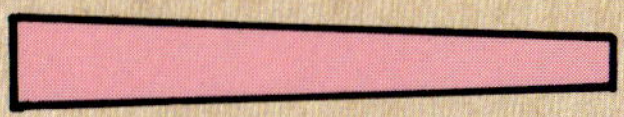	16in (40cm)	1/2in (1.5cm) tapering to 3/8 in (1cm)

The dimensions given are for beads made from sugar paper. For thicker paper, shorten strip length. For thinner paper, lengthen strip. Make up a few test beads every time you try a new kind of paper. For economical use of paper, position bead strips top to tail.

Make a bead drying rack from a shoe box lid. String the beads on knitting needles or lengths cut from wire coathangers.

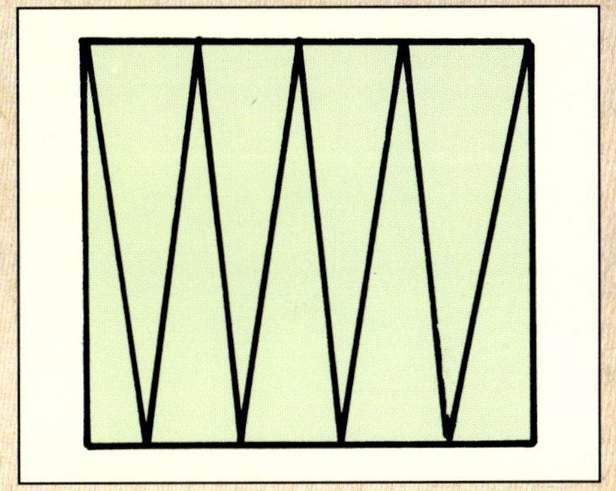

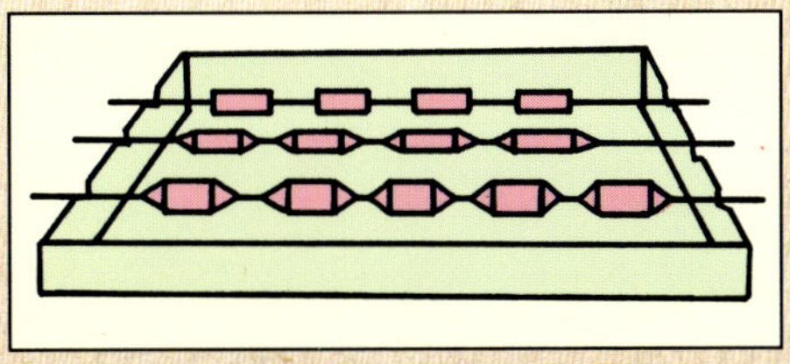

CUTTING

Refer to the bead shape chart. Mark bead patterns on paper. If you position identical bead patterns head to tail, there will be no paper waste. Cut the strips out using a scalpel and straightedge on a protected surface.

ROLLING

Use drinking straws, toothpicks or lengths of wire coathangers as rolling tools.

Start with the wide end of triangular strips and coil each bead strip around the tool, keeping the strip centred and maintaining an even tension. Glue end.

If desired, decorate the beads. Use felt tips, dimensional fabric paints or glued paper cut-outs. We use special decorative paper edging scissors to make cut-out strips, which were then glued on to the bead.

FINISHING

Seal the beads with lacquer, you may wish to apply a second coat. If your beads are decorated with felt-tip, test first to see if lacquer will make the colour run. String the beads when they are dry. Space the beads apart by knotting the co

CHAPTER THIRTEEN

ORIGAMI

As you probably know, origami is the Japanese art of paper folding. In Japan, origami is very much a part of daily life. For example, Japanese etiquette demands that gift parcels must be adorned with symbolic folded gift tags called 'noshi', which vary according to the gift.

In western culture, origami is widely regarded as a children's pastime or a party entertainment. Its adult following is growing, however, as a wider public learns to appreciate the beauty and ingenuity of origami as an art form.

In origami, a piece of paper (usually square) is folded into a representational figure or decorative shape. Purists permit no cutting, gluing or drawn embellishment. In addition, a 3D model should be able to fold down flat.

There is some basic terminology to learn:
A valley fold is a fold towards you.
A mountain fold is a fold away from you.
A squash fold involves folding and then squashing the paper to crease it.
A reverse fold can be either inwards or outwards.

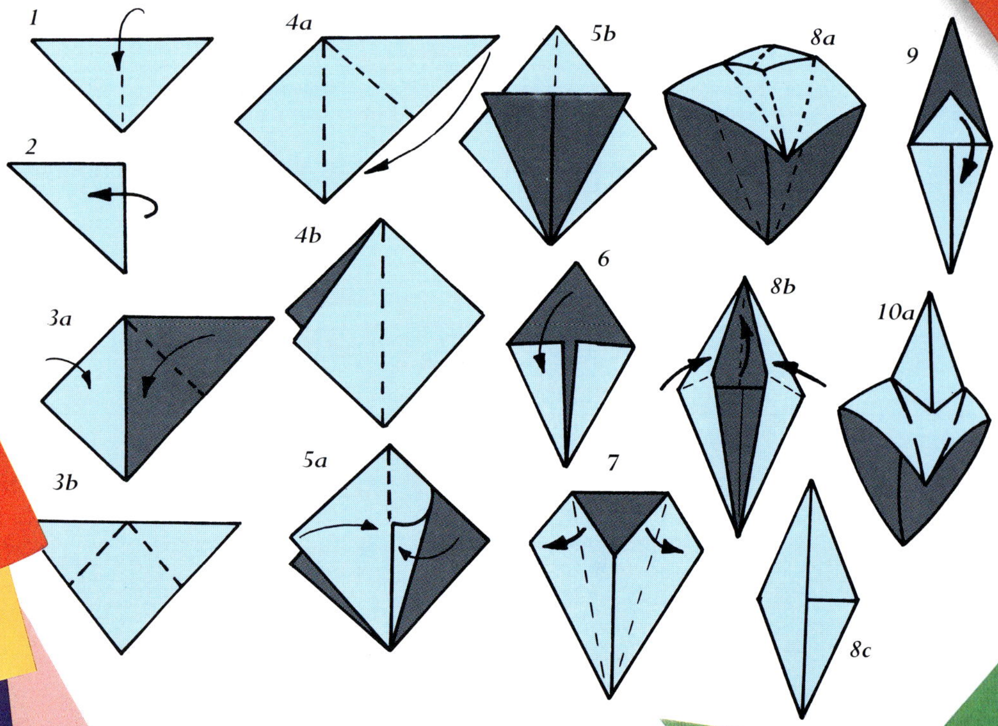

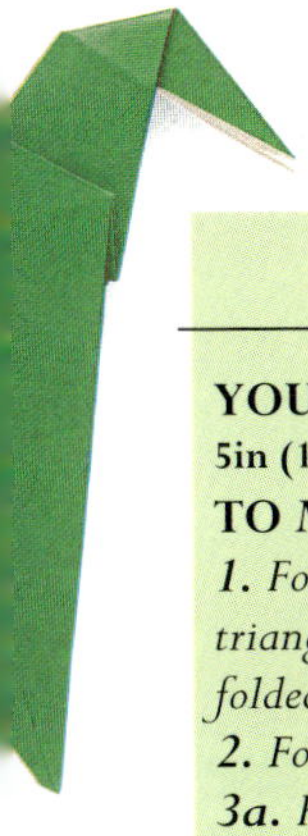

ORIGAMI BIRD

YOU WILL NEED:
5in (13cm) square of origami paper

TO MAKE UP:

1. *Fold square in half diagonally to form a triangle (white side of paper is inside the folded triangle).*

2. *Fold triangle in half sideways. Open out.*

3a. *Fold top corners down to meet at bottom point, then,*

3b. *open out.*

4. a and b. *Tuck in top triangles to form the preliminary bird base.*

5 a and b. *Fold right and left open edges to centre, forming a kite shape Now turn the paper over and repeat steps 5a and 5b.*

6. *Fold the top triangle down, then back up again.*

7. *Open out the right and left flaps from beneath the top triangle.*

8 *a,b and c. Pick up the bottom point (8a), gently pulling it backwards until it is level with your worksurface (8b). As if by magic, a diamond shape has formed (8c). Crease the diamond flat.*

9. *Turn the paper over. Crease the triangle down. Repeat step 7.*

10. *a, b and c. Repeat steps 8 a, b and c. The resulting double-sided diamond shape is called a bird base.*

11. *Fold the top diamond-point down to the middle crease . (The newly-formed triangle will be the bird's head and beak.)*

12.*a and b. Turn the top right flap over to the left, as if closing a door (12a). Shape 12b is the result.*

13. *a and b. Turn the paper over and repeat steps 12 a and b.*

14. *Your folded shape should now look like this. The pointy peak will become the bird's tail, the flat-top peak, the bird's neck.*

15. *Fold the uppermost bottom triangle up to meet the tail-point. This forms a wing. Turn the shape over and repeat this step, to make other wing.*

16. *Grasp the bird's tail and gently pull it downwards into position indicated by the broken lines. Crease it firmly in place.*

17. *Pull down bird's neck, repeating step 16.*

18. *Reach inside the bird's neck and pull out the beak formed in step 11.*

19. *To make the bird flap, grasp bottom of neck and tug the tail backwards and forwards.*

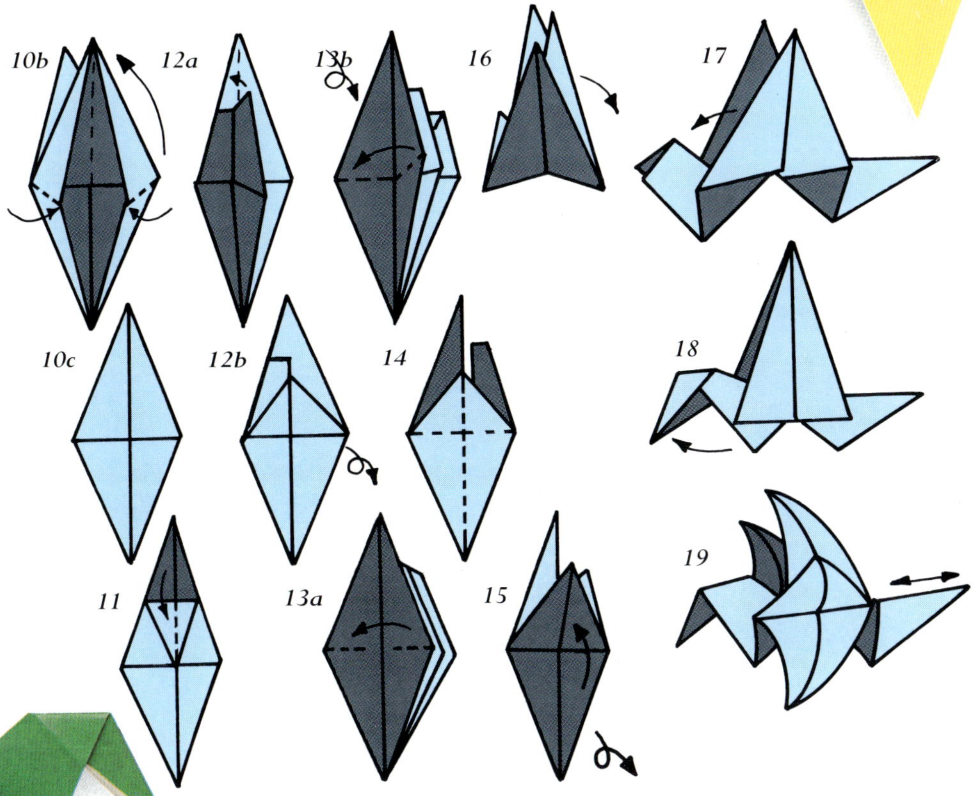

Origami Mobile

The Japanese regard the crane as a symbol of peace and good fortune. The crane model itself is a bit tricky for a novice, so we have substituted an easier bird. Follow the diagrams to master the model, then make this graceful circular mobile.

Birds In Flight Mobile

YOU WILL NEED:
8 pieces of 6in (15cm) square Origami paper • Inner ring from an 8in (20cm) diameter embroidery hoop • 2yds (2m) of 1/4in (6mm) wide white ribbon • A curtain ring • Yellow crêpe paper • Fine-gauge fishing line • High-tack craft adhesive • Straight pins • Large-eyed embroidery needle • Scalpel • Metal ruler • Scissors • Measuring tape • Clear adhesive tape • Masking tape

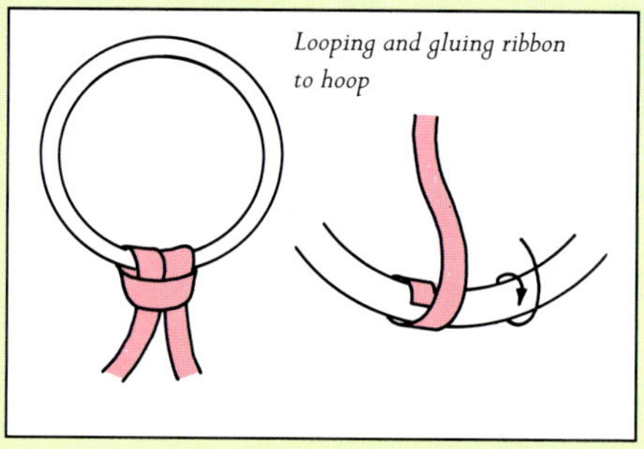

TO MAKE UP:

1. *Cut the Origami paper down into 5in (13cm) squares. Make up eight Flapping Birds, following folding diagrams on previous pages. You need two each of blue, yellow, orange and green.*

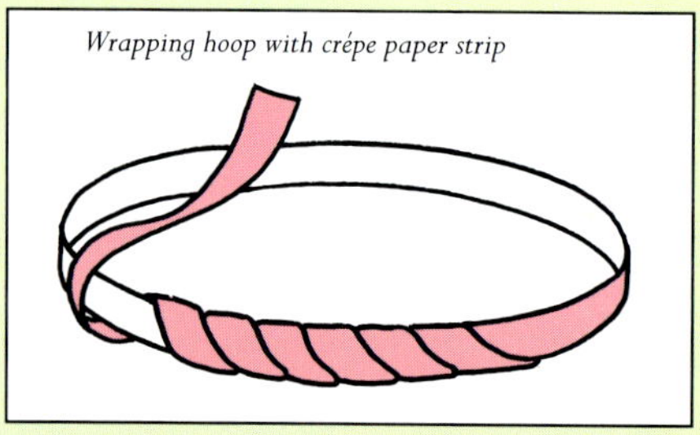

2. *To prepare the hoop, cut across a pack of crêpe paper, forming 1in (2.5cm) wide strips. Glue strip end inside hoop, then spiral strip around hoop to cover. Glue crêpe paper strip ends together, making one continuous strip. Glue end of strip inside hoop.*

3. *Measure the circumference of the hoop with the measuring tape, divide into eight. Mark eight equal divisions of the hoop by carefully piercing the crêpe paper with straight pins at appropriate places.*

4. *Cut two 24in (60cm) long ribbon strips. Stack one ribbon on top of the other, fold in half, then thread centre loop through curtain ring, making a half-hitch knot. Glue the ribbon ends to the hoop with high-tack glue at 'quarter hour' positions. Take care not to twist ribbon.*

5. *Cut eight lengths of fishing line to the following lengths plus 8in (20cm): 6in(15cm), 8in (20cm), 10in (25cm), 12in (30cm), 14in (35cm), 16in (40cm), 18in (45cm), 20in (50cm). Knot the end of each piece of fishing line, wrapping each knot with a piece of sticky tape (this prevents knot pulling through top of bird).*

6. *Thread needle with free end of fishing line, then pass needle through bird back point, tugging gently so knot settles beneath apex. Make sure you thread the correct length of line through the appropriate bird (see photograph).*

7. *When all the birds are threaded, measure the distance for fishing line from top of bird back upwards. Mark the distance at free end of line with a narrow snippet of masking tape.*

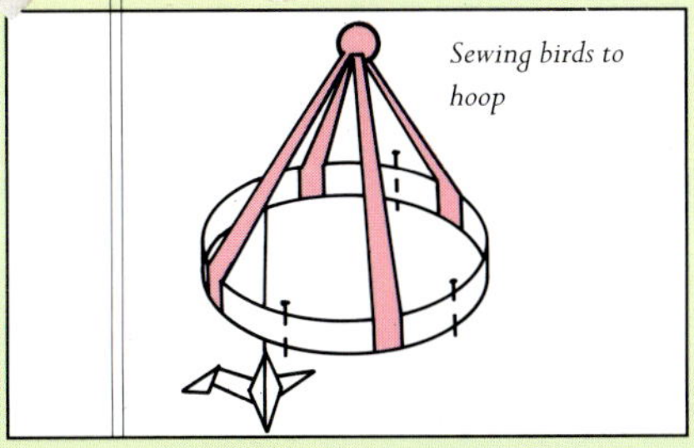

Sewing birds to hoop

8. *Thread needle onto each piece of line in turn, then sew birds, in sequence, onto wrong side of hoop at marked pin positions. The masking tape markers should be level with hoop.*

9. *Sew birds on in order of increasing line length; knot line ends.*

10. *Trim line close to each knot. When you finish sewing, carefully remove masking tape and dab on a drop of PVA glue to seal each knot. Also dab PVA glue onto the tip of each bird back.*

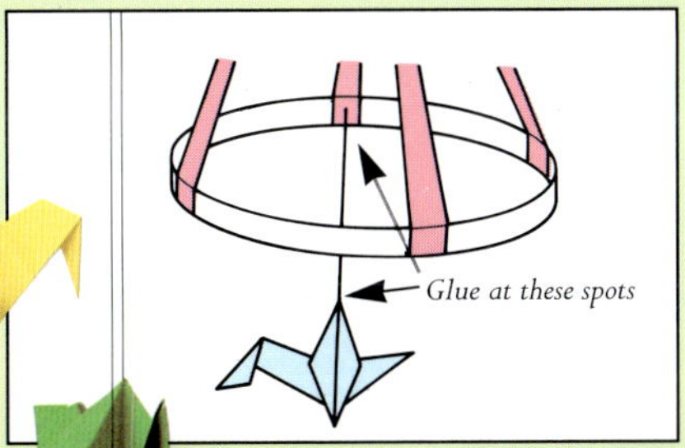

11. *Cut four 8in (20cm) pieces of ribbon, tie into bows, and glue on top of each end of ribbon on hoop, as shown.*

12. *Hang mobile from a cup hook, or tie another piece of fishing line onto curtain ring and suspend from a ceiling-height object.*

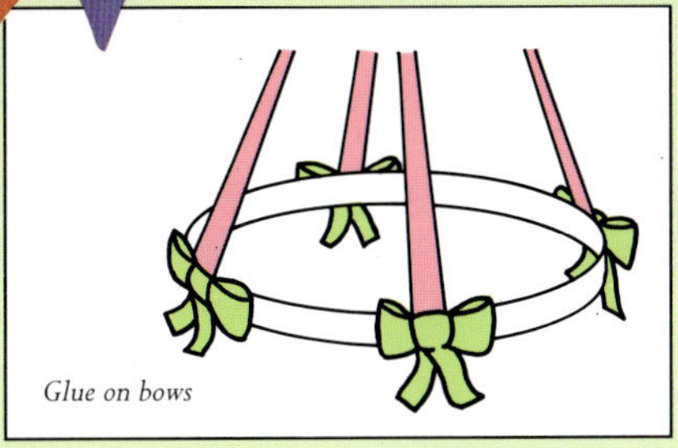

Glue on bows

Papier Mâché

Papier Mâché is a magical technique. A true economy craft, it enables you to create a permanent object of beauty out of nothing more than paper and glue. Painted and varnished, papier mâché objects look like ceramics.

The term papier mâché is French for 'chewed-up paper', and refers to the pulped paper 'mash' used for the process. The term also covers the newer, but more familiar, torn strip method of building up an object over a mould.

Torn Strip Method

For ***The Torn Strip Method*** *you will need:*
Torn strips of paper • PVA adhesive or wallpaper paste • Shallow dish for holding paste • Flat paintbrush • A smooth mould (such as a bowl, a balloon, or a ball) • Release agent: petroleum jelly or non-stick cooking spray • Blunt knife • Scissors • Sandpaper. For decoration: designer's gouache, poster colours, or acrylics • artist's paintbrushes.For sealing: clear polyurethane varnish

SELECT A MOULD

The mould determines the shape of the finished object. A bowl is a good first choice; paper strips can be applied inside or outside. Other possibilities include balloons and cardboard boxes. If a balloon is used, rest it in a support, such as a saucepan.

PAPER CHOICE

The paper must be porous to soak up the glue. Newspaper is cheap and easy to work with, but it deteriorates rapidly. Use it for your early attempts, but not for serious, permanent projects.

PAPER PREPARATION

Tear the paper into lengthwise strips, then tear the strips, crosswise, into pieces. Use large strips for covering big objects and smaller ones for smaller objects. Do not cut the paper strips, tearing the paper feathers the edges; this camouflages the joins.

THE GLUE MIXTURE

Dilute PVA adhesive, three parts glue to one part water; mix to a creamy consistency. Alternatively, use ready-mixed wallpaper paste.

PASTING

Coat the mould with release agent. Lay down the first layer of strips (it will temporarily stick), then brush on the paste mixture. Apply the second layer in the normal way, individually brushing the underside of each paper strip with the glue mixture. Leave the papier mâché to dry every three or four layers. A bowl requires about eight to ten layers.

FINISHING

When the papier mâché is dry it will sound hard when you tap it with your finger. Gently prise off the mould, using a blunt knife. Smooth rough spots with fine sandpaper. Trim rough edges with scissors. You may wish to smooth off the cut edge by pasting on two layers of folded-over paper strips.

Decorate the object with paint. Give your project two coats of base colour before applying the design. When dry, seal with a protective coating of varnish or dilute PVA mixture.

Fruit

These fabulous fakes are made by the torn strip method.

YOU WILL NEED:
Newspaper strips • PVA adhesive • Card • Masking tape • Scissors • Paints: designer's gouache, poster colours or acrylics; • Paintbrush • Fine sandpaper • Varnish.

WATERMELON

1. *To make the basic shape, create an armature, a support that remains inside the papier mâché shape. Draw a circle onto a piece of card. Cut it out, then cut it in half. Tape together along straight edges and stuff the wedge with crumpled newspaper to make the rounded bottom of the melon. Use masking tape to secure the newspaper filling.*
2. *Apply the papier mâché strips. Stick newspaper strips dipped in diluted PVA onto the watermelon base, building it up until the desired shape is achieved.*
3. *Leave to dry overnight. Sand any rough areas, if necessary.*
4. *Devise armatures for the other pieces of fruit. Crescent-shaped pieces of card become a banana; small balls of crumpled newspaper - cherries. Build up an apple shape from a larger ball of crumpled newspaper.*
5. *Cover with paper strips in the same way as the watermelon.*
6. *Paint the fruit, using the illustrations (or real fruit) as a guide.*
7. *Finish with a coat of varnish.*

The bold shapes and bright colours of fruit are perfect for papier mâché modelling

CHAPTER
• FOURTEEN •

Mash Method

Pulped papier mâché is clay-like in behaviour. Using paper pulp is a more efficient way to create bulk than the layered strip method.

Mash differs from true clay in that it usually requires an in-built support , or armature. Mash can be applied onto a plasticine mould (a mask-making technique), or it can be spread onto an armature. Chicken wire covered in aluminium foil,a cardboard box or tubing, a piece of polyboard or corrugated card - any or all of these things can make a good permanent armature.

Using an armature cuts the amount of pulp required for a project, reducing drying time.

It is possible to purchase a prepared mash mixture from craft shops. Just add water and mix. If you prefer to make your own, here's how.

*For **The Mash Method** you will need:*
Pulped paper • Large mixing bowl • PVA adhesive • Dry wallpaper paste • Liquidizer • Wooden mixing spoon • Strainer or colander • Linseed oil • Oil of cloves • Mould or armature • Release agent: petroleum jelly, non-stick cooking spray • Fine sandpaper • Acrylic primer or gesso, paintbrush • Polyurethane varnish

PREPARE THE PULP

Tear paper into ½ in (1cm) squares. Fill a large bowl with the torn paper pieces, and hot water just to cover; soak overnight. Whizz the mixture in a liquidizer, pulping it in small batches. Strain the pulp.

ADD THE BINDER

Mix in ½ pt (250ml) of PVA glue. Also add a little dry wallpaper paste, to improve the texture. Stir until a stiff and mushy consistency, like creamy mashed potatoes, is achieved.

A couple of tablespoons of linseed oil makes pulp smoother and acts as a hardener.

Add a few drops of oil of cloves (available from chemists) as a preservative. Mash can be stored in plastic bags in a refrigerator.

WORKING WITH THE MASH

If a plasticine or other removable mould is being used, coat it with releasing agent before applying the mash. (Releasing agent is not needed for a permanent armature). Spread the mash, pressing it into any depressions. Let mash dry slightly, then smooth it with the bowl of a spoon. Small details can be added.

FINISHING

When thoroughly dry, sand the finished piece. Seal with primer before painting - either two coats of gesso or one of acrylic primer. Decorate the papier mâché, applying two coats of the base colour. Add a final layer of polyurethane varnish.

POT POURRI BOWL

YOU WILL NEED:

Prepared paper pulp • Pot pourri • Template bowl • Petroleum jelly • Water-based paints/inks • Paintbrush • Knife • Varnish.

1. Smear petroleum jelly on inside of bowl.
2. Press the pot pourri onto the sides of the bowl. The petroleum jelly will keep it in place.

3. Press the prepared pulp mixture evenly over the pot pourri taking it about 1/2 inch over the top of bowl for a raggy, organic look.
4. Leave the papier mâché bowl to almost dry out, then slip a knife around the edge and gently lever it out. If any pot pouri falls off stick it back on using PVA or wallpaer adhesive.
5. Paint the bowl in the colours of your choice. You could dribble the inks on the inside of the bowl to give a marbled look. Leave to dry, then coat with two coats of varnish.

CHAPTER • FOURTEEN •

Paper Casting

Currently fashionable, paper casting is the craft of moulding relief designs using thick paper pulp. Unlike papier mâché mash, pulp for paper casting has no added glue, and so dries to a matt finish. You can make a small decorative cast-paper plaque using the mould supplied with this Workstation. Use it for decorating gift packages.

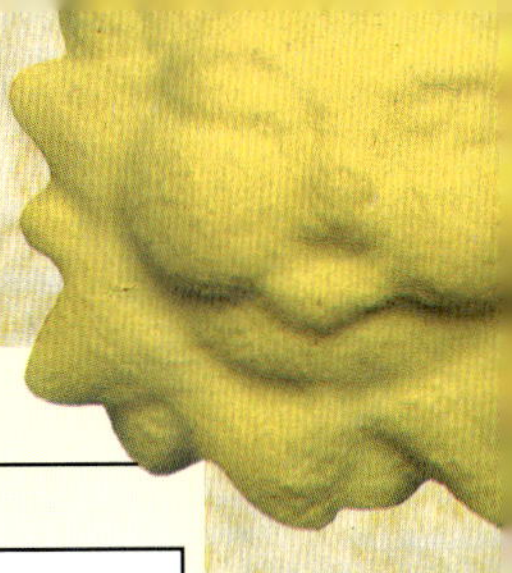

CAST PAPER PLAQUE

YOU WILL NEED

Sun mould (supplied in your Workstation) • 1 sheet of paper from back of book • Paints (supplied) • paintbrush • A liquidizer • Plasticine • Blunt table knife • strainer. Optional: • PVA adhesive • Narrow ribbon • Greeting card blank • Double sided sticky-back mounting tabs.

1. Soak one sheet of the special paper for two minutes in a liquidizer filled with 1 litre of cold water.

Special paper crumpled in 1 litre of water in liquidizer

2. Whizz liquidizer on high speed for one minute.

3. To anchor the mould onto your worksurface, set it in a piece of plasticine.

Mould fixed in plasticine

4. Strain off approximately one third of the water, then fill the mould with the pulped paper, just to cover. Distribute the cotton pulp evenly, levelling it with a blunt knife and filling all the recesses. Using your fingers, squeeze off as much excess water as possible. If you prefer, leave the pulp to run outside the mould, creating a ragged edge or deckle.

Levelling the pulp

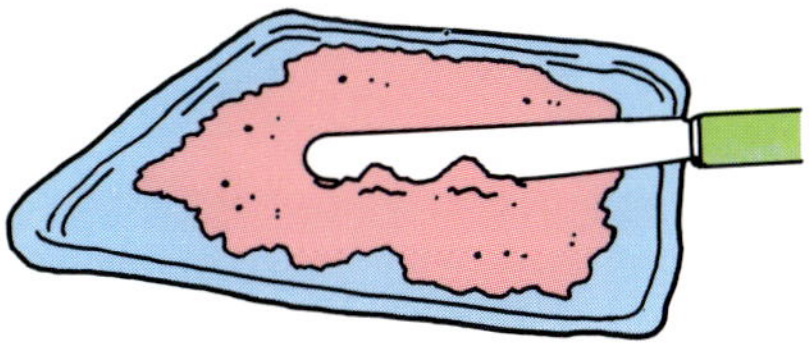

Mould drying in sun

5. Dry them in a warm place.

6. When the cast paper is thoroughly dry, gently slide a dull knife around under the deckle to prise the edges free, then turn out the mould.

7. If you wish, decorate the cast-paper plaque with the paints supplied.

8. You can use your sun as a decoration simply by suspending it from a piece of pretty string. Alternatively, use it as a giftwrap tag-style decoration.

Decorating motif

Paper Containers

Box-making and paper basketry provide an ideal creative opportunity for the ecology-conscious papercrafter. What could be better than to package a gift in a re-usable container that has been constructed from recycled materials? The packaging itself is an appreciated gift!

Boat-Shaped Basket

YOU WILL NEED:
Corrugated card • Cardboard carton card • Paper twist • Awl or nail • Tapestry needle • Scalpel • Metal ruler • Scissors • PVA adhesive.

TO MAKE UP:

1. The basket consists of four pieces - the base, two sides and the handle. The base pattern and side cutting diagrams are in the back of the book. Enlarge the base pattern and cut it out from cardboard carton card.

2. Cut two identical slotted side units from corrugated card.

3. For the handle, cut a strip of corrugated card 22in (55cm) long by 1 1/4in (3.5cm) wide.

4. To assemble the basket, hold one side panel with slots upwards, the other with slots downwards. Slot them together.

5. Apply PVA glue all round the basket base sides. Slide the side panels over the base, matching points - it should be a snug fit. Pipe PVA glue all round the basket base interior, using it as a sealant where the sides meet the base. Leave to dry.

6. Glue the handle to the inside of the basket sides. Pierce holes as marked.

7. Cut a narrow, 14in (35cm) long piece of paper twist and thread needle with it. Stitch a giant cross stitch on either side of basket. Glue down ends of paper twist.

'Stack of Sticks' Hexagon Basket

YOU WILL NEED:
Cardboard carton card • Scalpel • Metal ruler • Pencil • Protractor • PVA adhesive

1. For the basket, cut 60 sticks from card, each measuring 1/2 in (1.5cm) wide by 5in (12cm) long.
2. The base is a 2 1/2 in (6cm) cardboard hexagon. Use the protractor to measure the 60 degree angle for each hexagon side.
3. To assemble the box, lay three sticks, centred lengthwise, along three alternate sides of the hexagon base. Stick edges should be level with base edges. Glue each stick to the base with dabs of glue.
4. For the next round, place centred sticks along the remaining hexagon sides. Glue sticks at contact points.
5. Continue in this way, edging sticks slightly outward with each new round. Build the basket up in this way for eight or ten rounds. Leave to dry.
6. You may wish to apply a protective coat of varnish to the finished basket, or to the individual sticks and base prior to gluing.

Beaded Plant Pot Cover

YOU WILL NEED:
Plastic flowerpot • Cardboard carton card • Coloured cartridge paper • Cocktail sticks, for beads • Needle and strong thread (such as button thread) • Scalpel • Metal ruler • Pencil • Measuring tape • PVA adhesive • Paper twist, for bow • Calculator (speeds up the arithmetic).

TO MAKE UP:
1. The height of each slat is the flowerpot height + 1/3in (1cm). Measure the circumference around flowerpot base. For a small flowerpot, divide this figure by 20; for a larger pot, divide by 25. This figure, probably between 1/3 and 1/2 in (1 and 1.5cm) is the width of each slat.
2. Cut slats from card. Pencil across each stick width, 1/3in (1cm) up from bottom and 1/2 in (1.5cm) below the top.
3. Measure the top circumference of the pot; write this figure down.
4. The paper cylinder beads for the top of the cover are rolled from cartridge paper strips (see Paper Beads, page 30). To determine the width of each bead, subtract the bottom circumference from the top circumference and divide by the number of slats in the pot cover. Make your cylinder beads 1/16 in (1mm) narrower than this measurement. Try 6in (15cm) for the length of each bead strip. As the beads require tiny holes, use cocktail sticks for your rolling tools. Make about 30 beads, so you can choose the best of the lot.
5. Thread a needle with heavy-weight thread and pass it through the base of each slat at the marked level, stringing the slats side-by-side.
6. Thread the needle with another length of thread, and string the top of the plant pot cover, alternating beads and slats.
7. When you have finished, lay the flowerpot on the wrong side of the cover, then tie thread ends securely together at top and bottom, fastening the pot cover.
8. Trim off thread, secure each end with a dab of PVA glue.
9. You may wish to varnish the pot cover slats to improve water resistance.
10. Tie on a paper twist bow as shown.

CHAPTER
• SIXTEEN •

Greetings Cards

Hand-crafted greetings cards have a personalised something extra no machine can imitate. And your original pop-ups have something extra plus – the element of surprise.

Cards and stationary are small-scale projects, and, as such, provide a golden opportunity to experiment with new techniques and materials, and you can go really wild with exuberant designs.

Greetings cards can either be one-off or part of a limited run of identical or similar cards.

Try out some of the simple printing techniques - stamping, stencilling, or paste - featured in this book. Handmade paper makes up into lovely cards and notes, but use bond paper lining sheets to provide a smooth writing surface.

Pop-ups are novelty surprise cards. Think about making cards with dials, fold-outs, pull-tabs, or flaps to lift. Browse in your local card shop for ideas.

Making your own envelopes frees you from working to standard card sizes. Open out existing envelopes to see how it is done. Seal with a glue stick.

Antique Fan Pop-Up

YOU WILL NEED:

Card • Paper • Scissors • Gold marker pen • Ribbon • Glue stick • PVA adhesive.

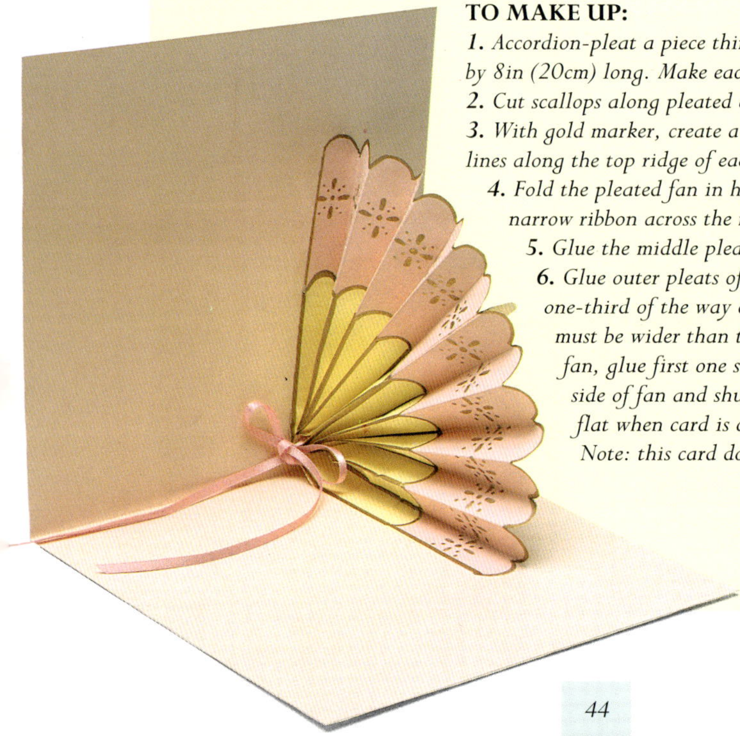

TO MAKE UP:

1. *Accordion-pleat a piece thin of paper about 7in (18cm) wide by 8in (20cm) long. Make each pleat ½ in (1.5cm) wide.*

2. *Cut scallops along pleated edges at top and bottom.*

3. *With gold marker, create a lacy fan decoration, and draw lines along the top ridge of each pleat.*

4. *Fold the pleated fan in half width wise, lay a piece of narrow ribbon across the midpoint (see photograph).*

5. *Glue the middle pleat together; tie ribbon into a bow.*

6. *Glue outer pleats of fan to either side of card, about one-third of the way down from card top. The card must be wider than the span of the fan. To glue the fan, glue first one side, then apply glue to the other side of fan and shut the card on it. The fan folds flat when card is closed.*

Note: this card does not open out fully.

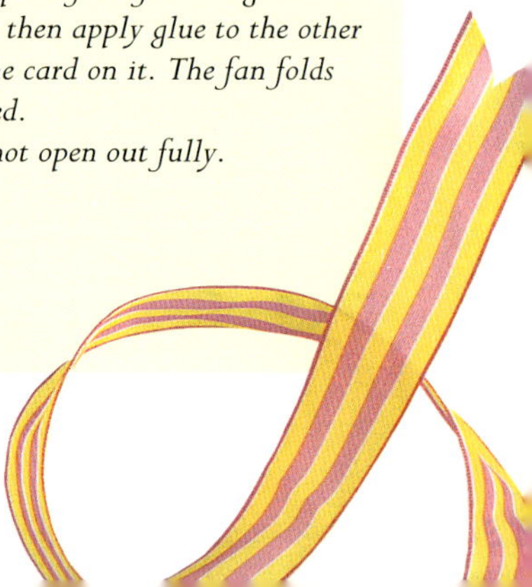

Flower Urn Pop Up

YOU WILL NEED:
Card • Coloured cartridge paper • Scissors • PVA adhesive • Glue stick • Pencil • Scalpel • Holepunch.

TO MAKE UP:

1. Trace off flower urn motif from the back of the book and make up the design with cut-outs stuck onto card.
2. Make flower centres and openwork on urn base with the holepunch.
3. Cut out the pop-up base, slitting and scoring it as indicated on the pattern.
4. For card cover: glue a piece of card, same size as pop-up base, onto back of base, but do not apply glue stick to area within slits.
5. Crease the centre fold of card and fold up the slit area to form a 'stair step'.
6. Glue the urn motif onto front section of stair step. Fold card flat. Urn pops up when card is opened.

Teddy Pop-Ups

YOU WILL NEED:
Card • Tan cartridge paper • Contrasting papers for ears, face, waistcoat etc • Scissors • Glue stick • PVA adhesive.

TO MAKE UP:

1. Cut a card base measuring 4in (10cm) high by 6in (15cm) wide (centre fold).
2. Trace off the teddy body pattern from the back of the book onto tan cartridge paper.
3. Trace ear centres, face oval, and dress or waistcoat onto contrasting-coloured paper; colour these in, then cut out. Stick cut-outs into appropriate position on each teddy (use a glue stick).
4. Bow/bowtie cut-outs are only glued to teddy at centres (use PVA).
5. Make criss-cross folds at arm level as marked on teddy pattern, then fold each teddy (right sides together) in half vertically. Tuck under teddy head along folds (see diagram at the back of the book).
6. Glue teddy paws to either side of card, near top. The teddy will open out when card is opened.
7. To display card, reverse the centre crease, so it faces outwards. Note: the card does not open out fully.

GIFTWRAPPING

Wrapping your gifts can be as pleasurable as receiving them! Paper and the art of giftwrapping were made for each other. Use the decorative techniques you have learned from this book to come up with ideas for gift wrapping.

Think of every gift as a problem to be solved. The ideal wrapping should be attractive and perfectly suited to the nature of its contents. For instance, if an object is large or unusually shaped, a gift sack may be the answer. Think before you wrap, and you won't go wrong.

Giftwrapping provides an excellent opportunity for recycling papers and cards. Cartons can be cut up and re-modelled into smaller boxes and containers. Bags can be made out of patterned giftwrap, as can paper ribbon and bows. Double-sided tape is handy for giftwrapping. Try it for attaching bows or ribbons invisibly - it's quicker and neater than glue. Use it sparingly, as it is pricey - but a little goes a long way.

Window Gift Boxes

YOU WILL NEED:
Coloured corrugated card
For windows: glassine paper or coloured cellophane • Thin white card, for tags • White cartridge paper (for seals) • Paper ribbon • Scalpel • Ruler • Scissors • Holepunch • Decorative edgers • PVA adhesive • Glue stick.

TO MAKE UP:
1. *Enlarge the box patterns from the back of the book, in the desired shapes and sizes. Copy each box pattern onto the smooth side of corrugated card, placing the straight box folds in the direction of the ridges.*

2. *For the gift tags, enlarge the shapes to a size smaller than that of the picture window.*
3. *Cut each box out, scoring as marked. Punch a hole at the right hand side of the box top flap.*
4. *For the gift tags, stick a piece of card onto the smooth side of the corrugated card (this is the writing surface).*
5. *Cut out the gift tag shapes and punch a hole in the top of each one.*
6. *Cut a piece of glassine (or cellophane) slightly larger all around than the window opening. On the smooth side of the card, apply glue all round the edge of the window opening. Smooth the glassine window covering onto the glue. Leave to dry.*
7. *Fold the box along the straight scored lines; glue the underlap. Leave to dry.*
8. *Tie the gift tag to the box with paper ribbon*

Glitzy Gift Boxes

Enlarge the hexagon box pattern in the back of the book into three graduated sizes.
Cut out and score the box bases and lids in co-ordinating colours of-coloured card.
Trace off the pattern motifs and cut them out in gold metallic paper. Glue the motifs, centred, onto the box lids and side panels, as shown. The box lid side panels are decorated with punched paper dots. It is easiest to apply decorations to the flat pattern pieces, before assembling the box. Make up the box bases and lids, folding and gluing as required.

Gift Wrap and Paper Bows

The giftwrap is simply drawn onto sheets of tissue paper using both plain and metallic felt-tips.
Trace off motifs from the back of the book and draw a master pattern the size of a sheet of tissue, in black permanent ink marker. Tape it onto a piece of card. Lay a sheet of tissue paper over this, securing it with snippets of masking tape all round. Trace the design onto tissue with the felt-tips. A simple design with flowing, repeating shapes can be reproduced quite quickly. Create your own design, or trace off our motifs .
Make gift tags to match the giftwrap. Make your own paper ribbon by cutting strips of metallic paper with decorative edgers. Glue ribbon onto the gift box.
To make bows, use edgers to cut four strips of thin card 8in (20cm) long by 1/2in (1.5cm)wide for each bow. Glue a centre strip of metallic paper onto each strip of card. Glue each strip into a loop. With loop overlap at centre, thread each loop in turn onto a paper fastener. Open out the fastener, then fan out the loops. Glue the bow onto the gift box.

Glossary

CORRUGATED CARD
Ridged packing material.

DECKLE
The irregular edge surrounding a piece of handmade paper.

FUSIBLE WEB
Iron-on adhesive suitable for bonding paper to card.

FOLD-AND-DYE
A paper decorating technique similar to tie-dye,in which paper is folded into a parcel and dipped in dye.

GRAIN
The directional orientation of fibres within a sheet of machine-made paper.

MARBLING
The process of creating decorative papers using paints which are floated on a bath of thickened water, and then arranged into swirling patterns.

MASH
Gluey paper pulp used for papier mâché sculpting.

ORIGAMI
The Japanese art of paper folding.

PAPIER MACHÉ
Literally (in French), 'chewed-up paper'. A wet papercraft technique in which either torn strips are pasted over a mould or paper pulp is formed over a mould or armature.

PAPER CASTING
The craft of moulding paper pulp, differing from papier mâché because of the absence of glue binder.

PASTE AND COMB PRINTING
A method of decorative printing using coloured starch paste which is scraped away using a stylus or comb.

PULP
Macerated paper and water, used for papermaking, paper casting and papier mâché.

QUILLING
Paper filigree, the craft of making ornamental scrollwork by coiling narrow strips of paper.

REGISTRATION
The proper alignment of printed shapes.

STAMPING
Printing method in which a raised surface is used to transfer pigment from one surface to another.

STENCILLING
Decorative printing method in which paint is applied to a cut-out area.

STONE
A droplet of dispersed paint on the surface of a marbling bath.

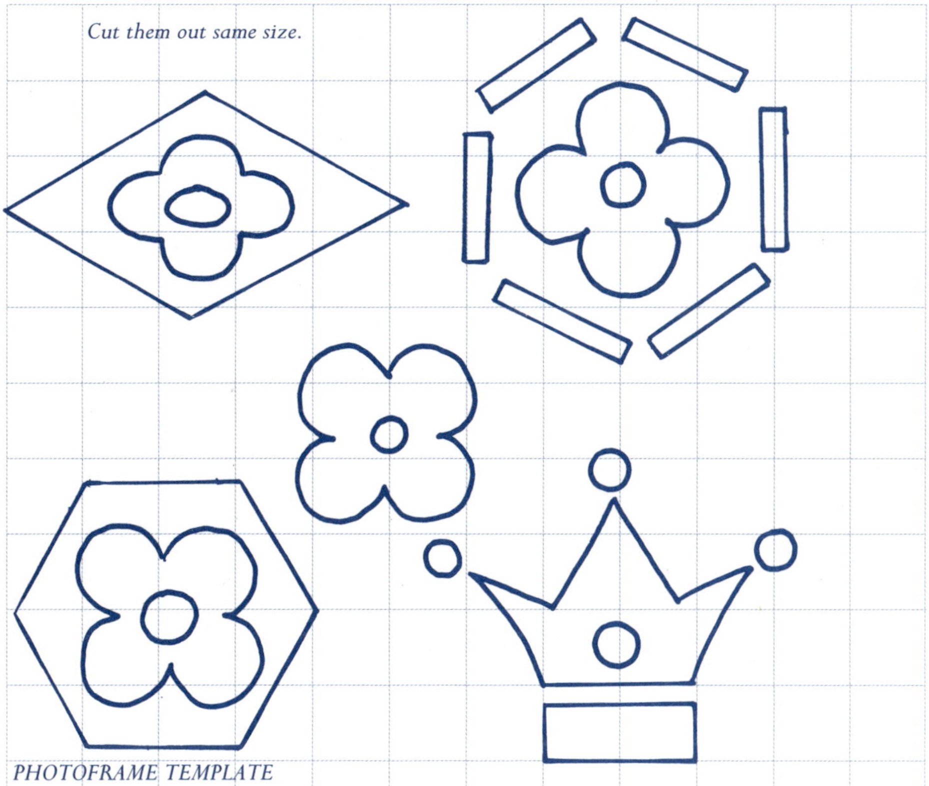

PHOTOFRAME TEMPLATE

1. Enlarge pattern by increasing size of each square to 15mm.
2. Cut out frame.
3. For corner tabs (paste and comb frame, page 15), draw a 1in (2.5cm) radius circle and cut into quarters.
4. Glue corner tabs in place, positioning straight tab edges 1/2in (1.5cm) in from the frame edges.
5. For photo insertion slots, cut through card along arcs.
6. Cut out strut and glue to frame back. Insert photo.

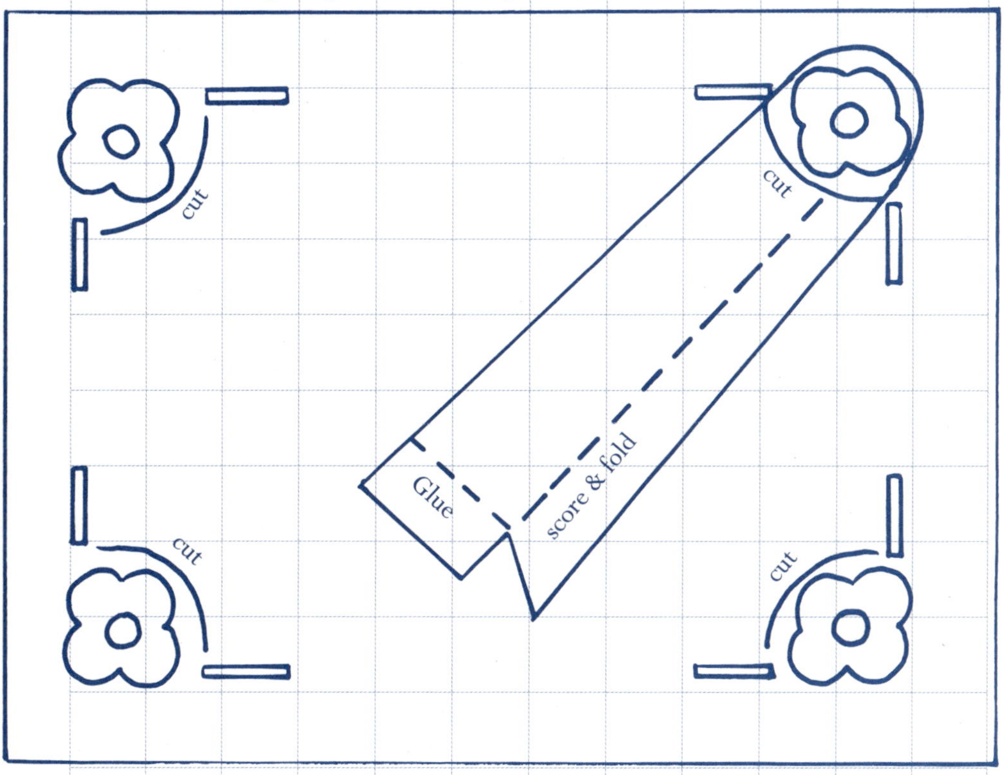

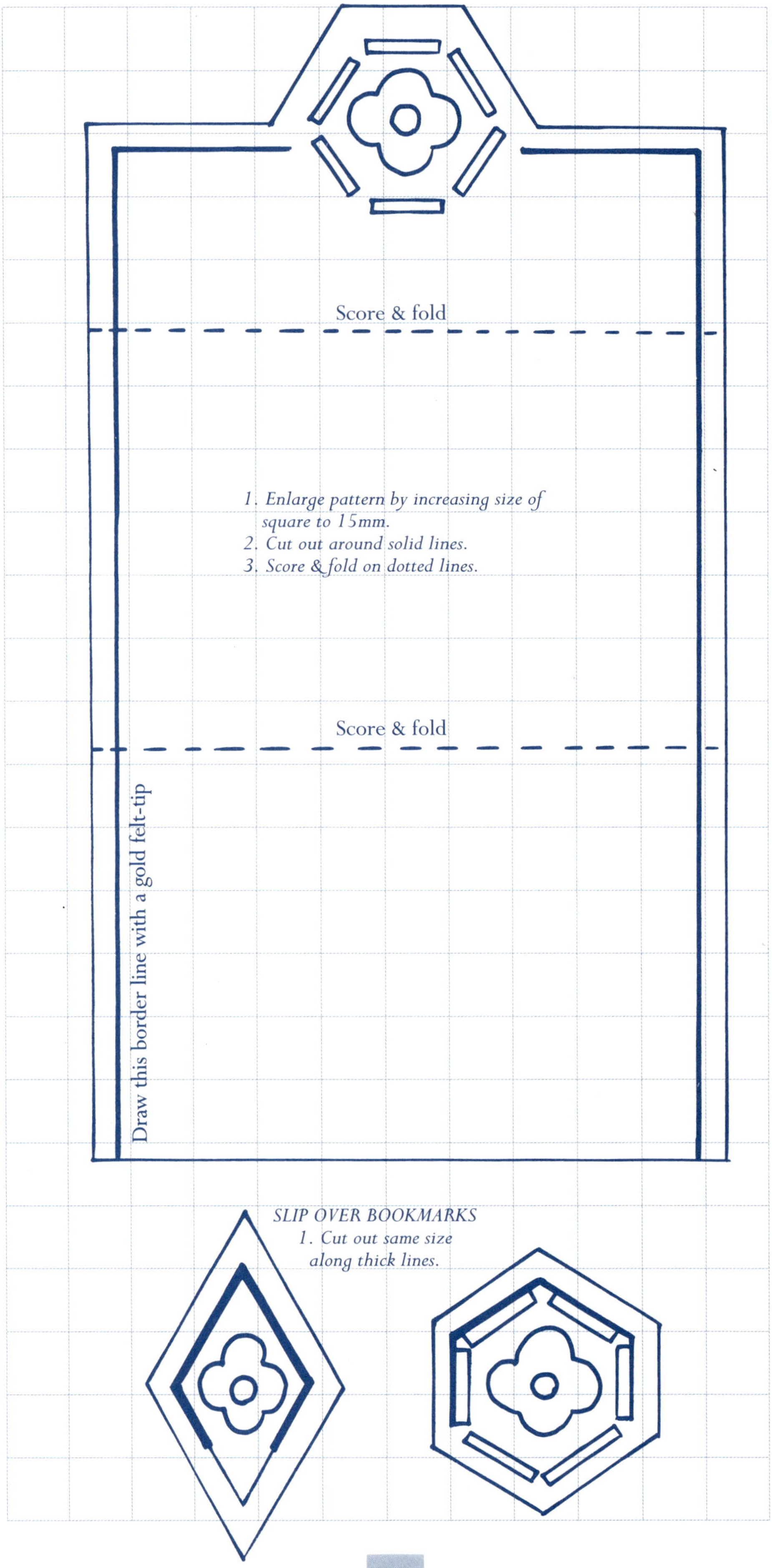
Score & fold
1. Enlarge pattern by increasing size of square to 15mm.
2. Cut out around solid lines.
3. Score & fold on dotted lines.
Score & fold
Draw this border line with a gold felt-tip
SLIP OVER BOOKMARKS
1. Cut out same size along thick lines.

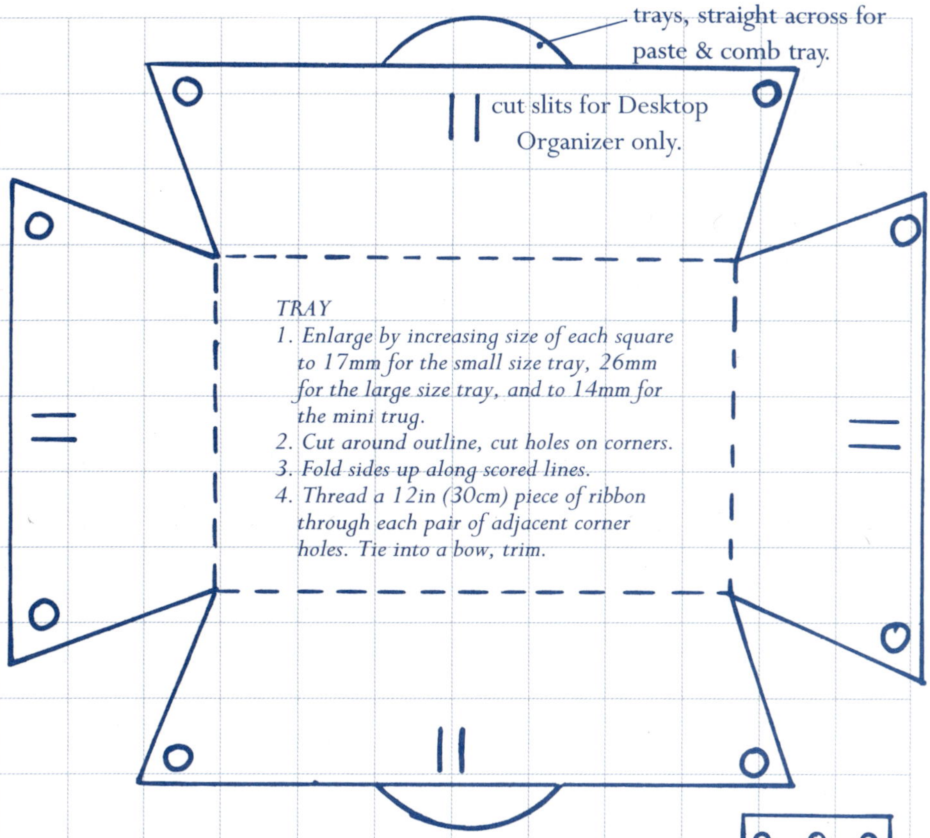

TRAY

1. *Enlarge by increasing size of each square to 17mm for the small size tray, 26mm for the large size tray, and to 14mm for the mini trug.*
2. *Cut around outline, cut holes on corners.*
3. *Fold sides up along scored lines.*
4. *Thread a 12in (30cm) piece of ribbon through each pair of adjacent corner holes. Tie into a bow, trim.*

LARGE BASKET HANDLE

1. *Enlarge by increasing size of each square to 26mm.*
2. *Cut out.*

MINI BASKET & TRUG HANDLE

Enlarge by increasing size of each square to 17mm

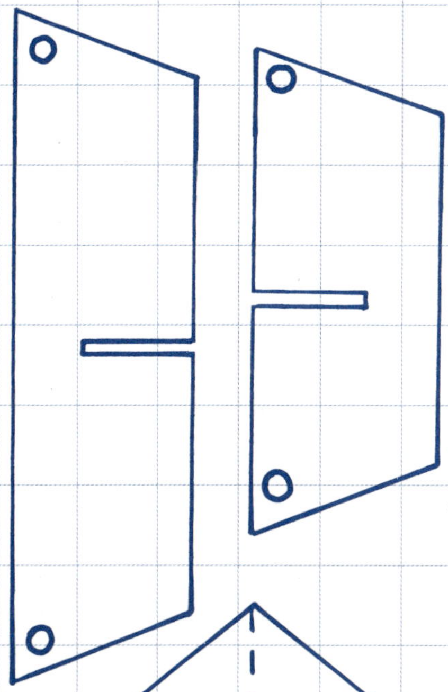

DIVIDERS

1. *Enlarge by increasing size of each square to 16mm and 14mm for the mini trug.*
2. *Cut out and join the slits together.*
3. *Thread a ribbon through the holes and through slits in the Tray above to secure them.*

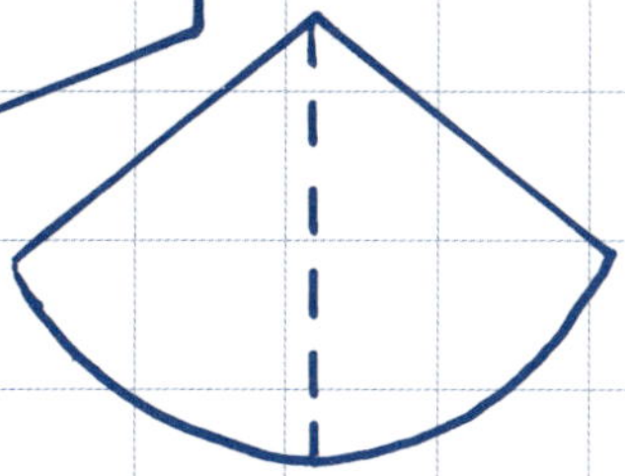

CORNER TABS FOR MARBLED ORGANIZER (*see page 20*)

1. *Decrease size of each square to 7.5mm for a small tray and increase to 16mm for a large tray.*
2. *You will need one for each corner.*
3. *Fold & glue onto outside of corners of tray*

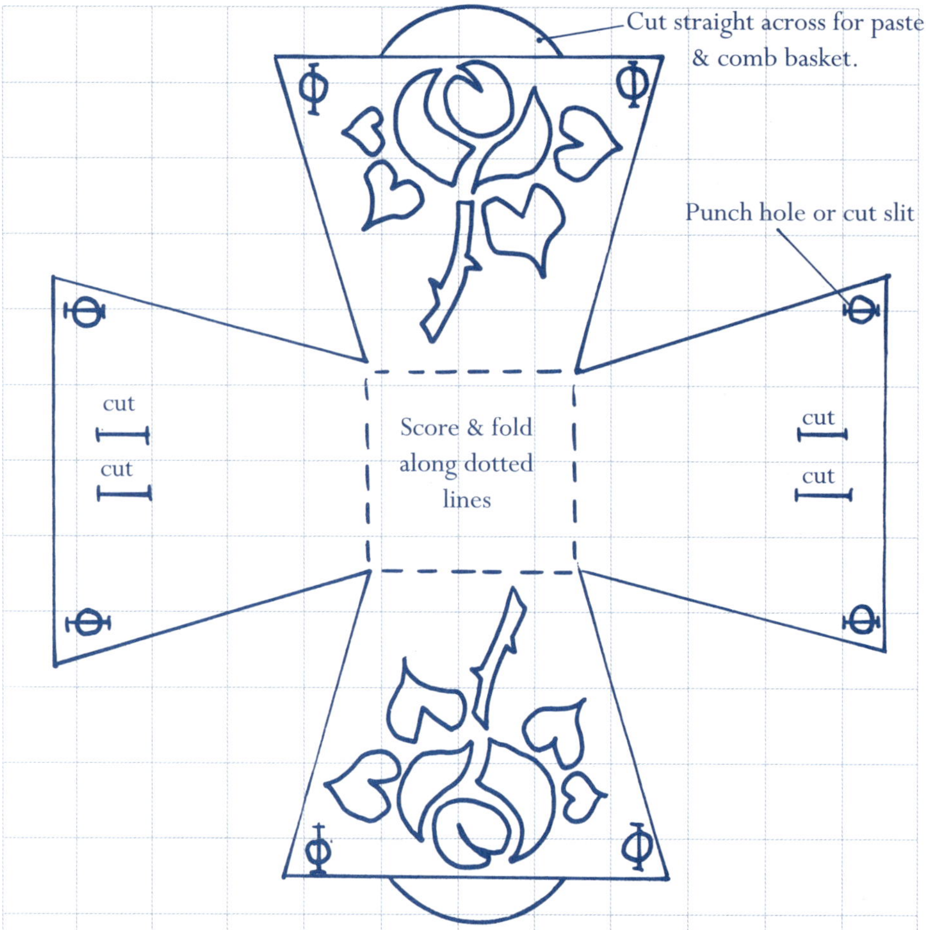

1. Enlarge by increasing size of each square to 18mm.
2. Cut out around outline.
3 Pierce holes in basket handle with an awl or nail (place a blob of plasticine underneath to receive the point).
4. Fold sides up and insert bows as for tray.
5. For the handle (pattern on page 3), knot a 27in (70cm) length of ribbon, thread it through handle hole (with knot on the wrong side). Spiral ribbon round handle, thread end through other hole, knot and trim.
6. Thread a 12in (30cm) length of ribbon through spiralled ribbon at each end of handle, tie into a bow.
7. Slot handle 'T-bars' into slits at basket sides.

ROSE STENCIL PATTERN AND PLACEMAT TEMPLATE

1. Enlarge by increasing each square to 40mm.

STAR & HEART ORNAMENTS

1. Enlarge by increasing each square to 16.6mm.

2. Cut out.

ROSE PARTYWARE NAPKIN RING

1. Enlarge by increasing each square to 20mm.

2. Overlap ends at back, glue in place.

CIRCULAR PAPERCUT PATTERN

Cut out same size

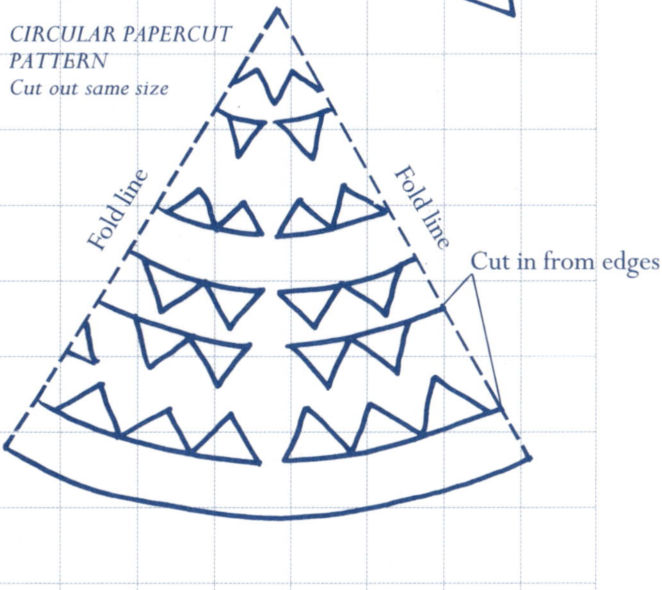

HEXAGON BOX MASTER TEMPLATE

Use for cut paper (page 23), quilling boxes (page 28), woven basket (page 27) or giftwrapping (page 46).

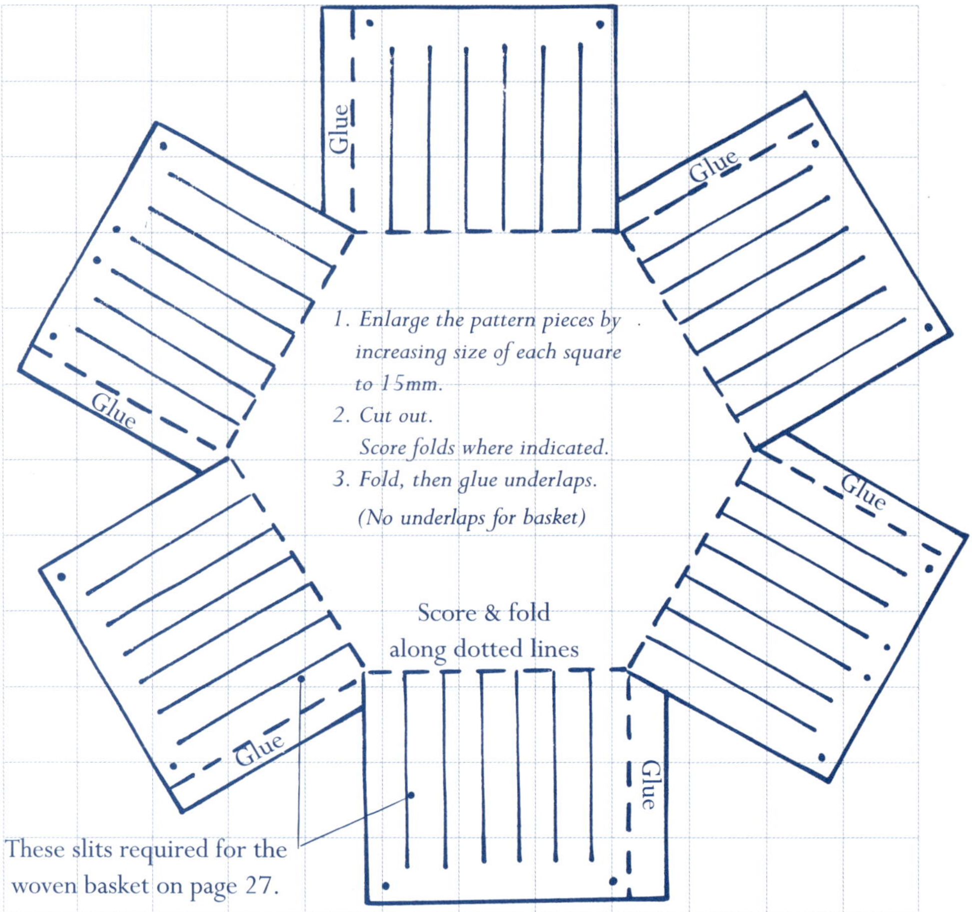

HEXAGON BOX LID TEMPLATE

1. Enlarge by increasing size of each square to 15mm.
2. Score & fold along dotted lines

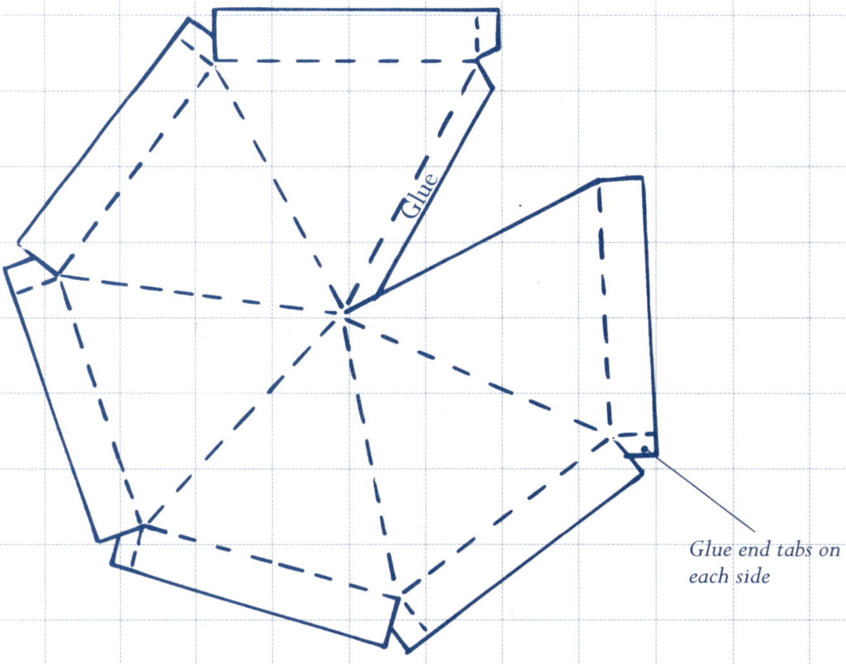

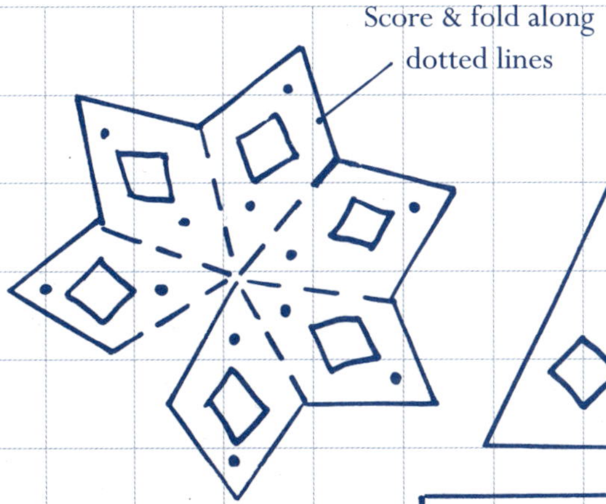

1. Cut out same size, along solid lines and make holes where indicated.
2. Glue onto the made up hexagon box.

FLOWER URN

1. Cut out same size.
2. Use with pop-up Greeting Card Template on page 15.

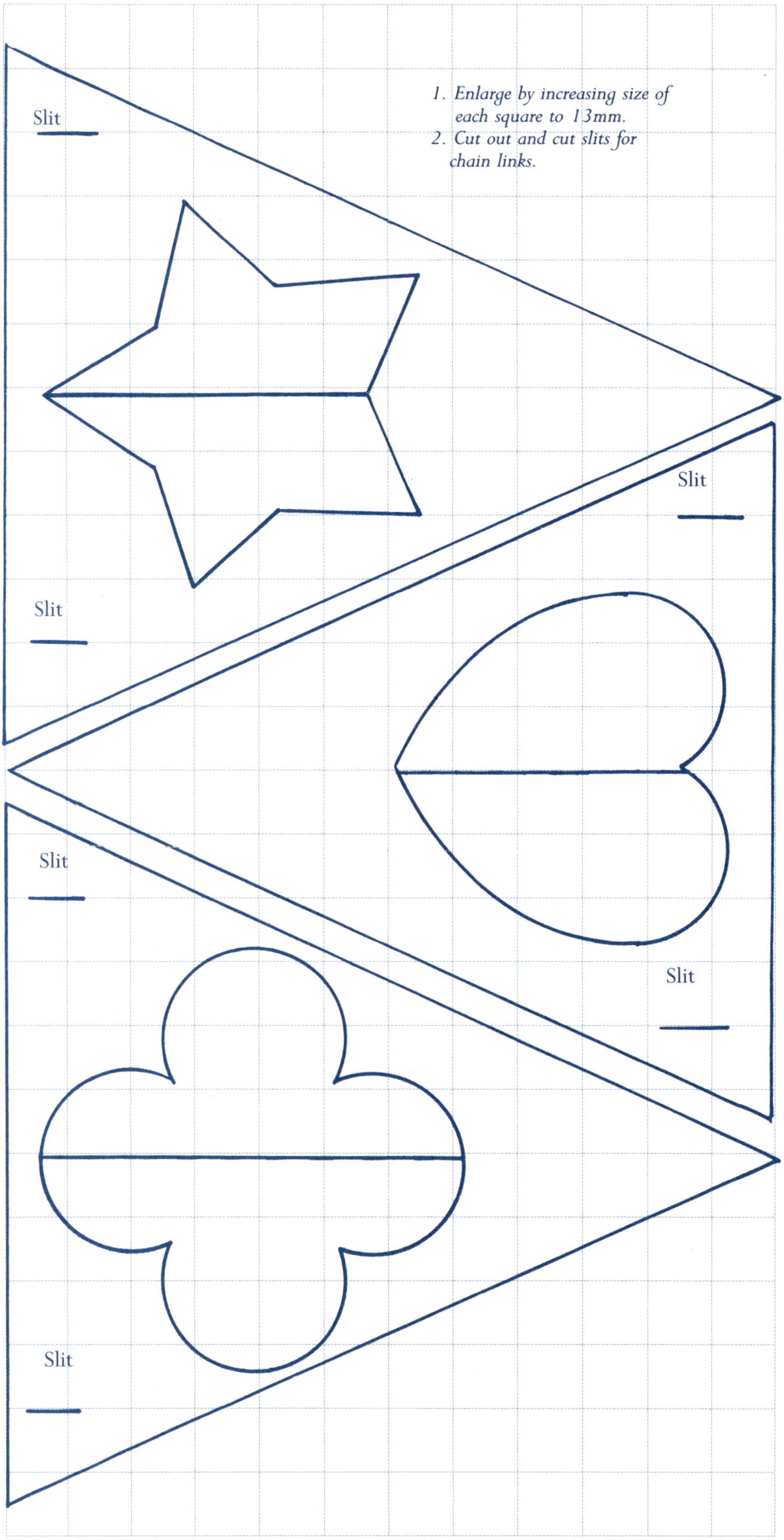

1. Enlarge by increasing size of each square to 13mm.
2. Cut out and cut slits for chain links.
Slit
Slit
Slit
Slit
Slit
Slit

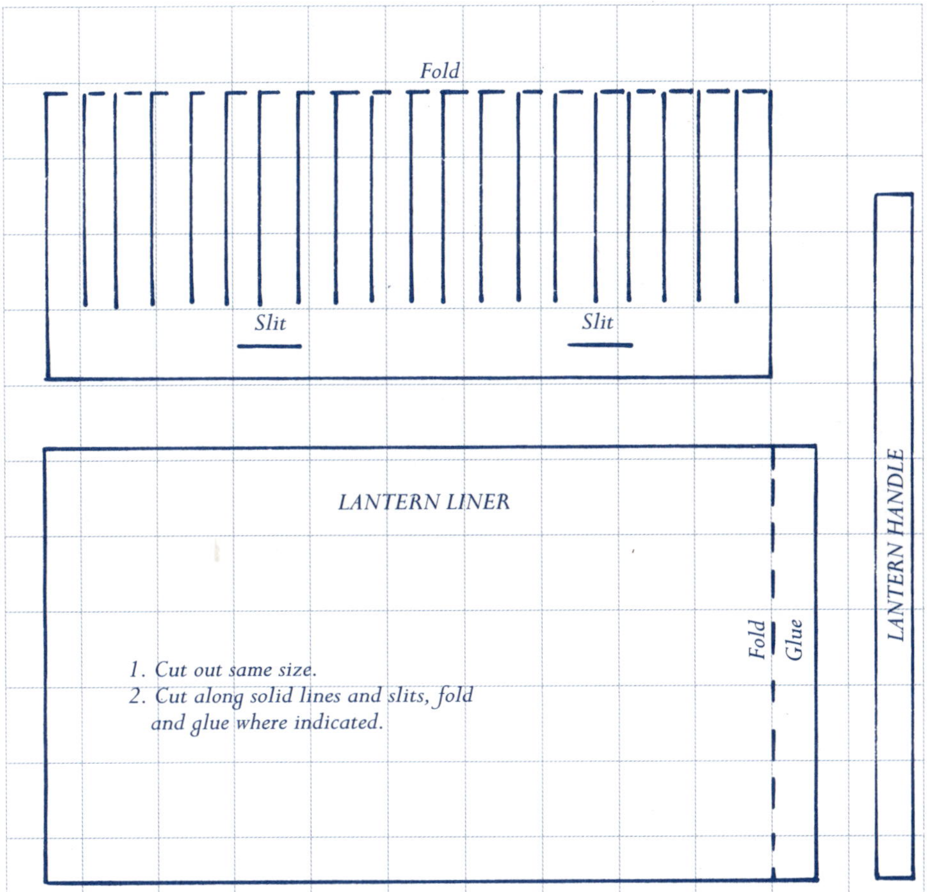
Fold
Slit
Slit
LANTERN LINER
1. Cut out same size.
2. Cut along solid lines and slits, fold and glue where indicated.
Fold
Glue
LANTERN HANDLE

3-D GARLAND

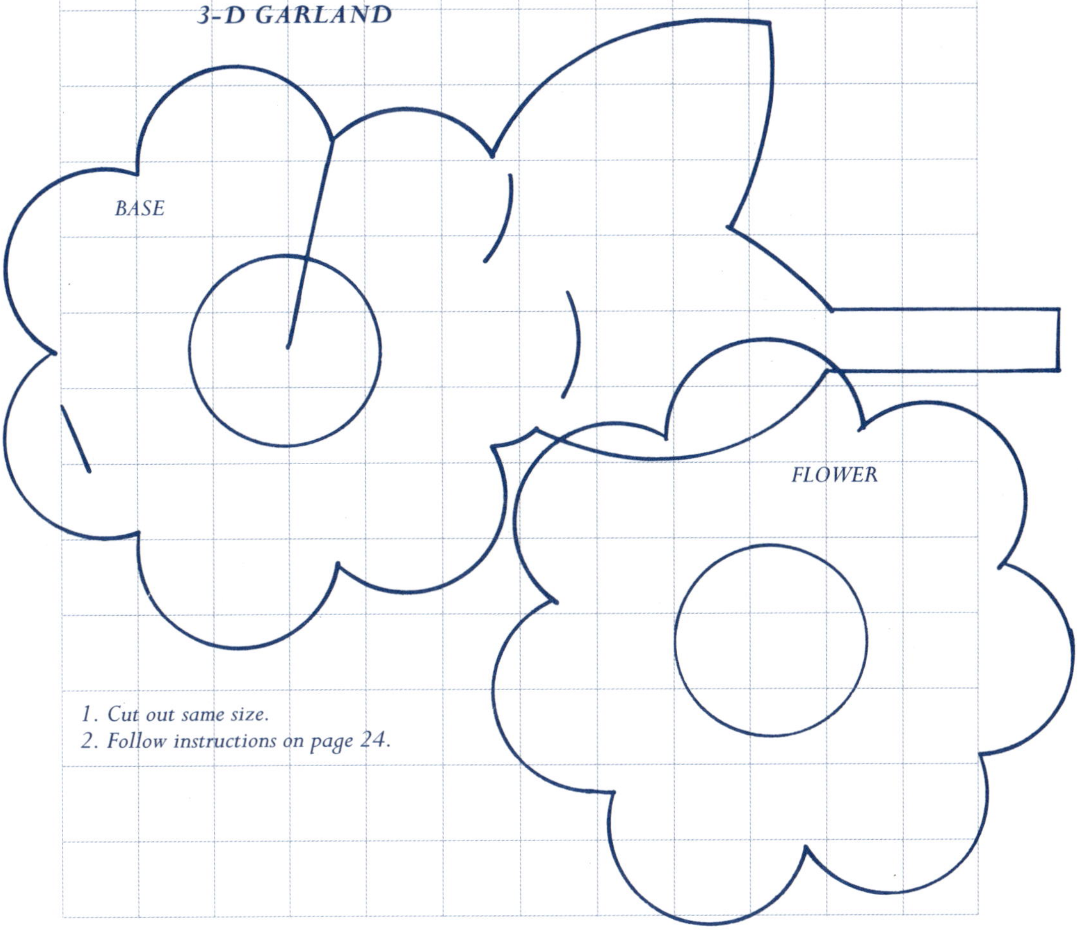
BASE
FLOWER
1. Cut out same size.
2. Follow instructions on page 24.

1. Cut out same size for large basket. For smaller basket each square = 75mm.

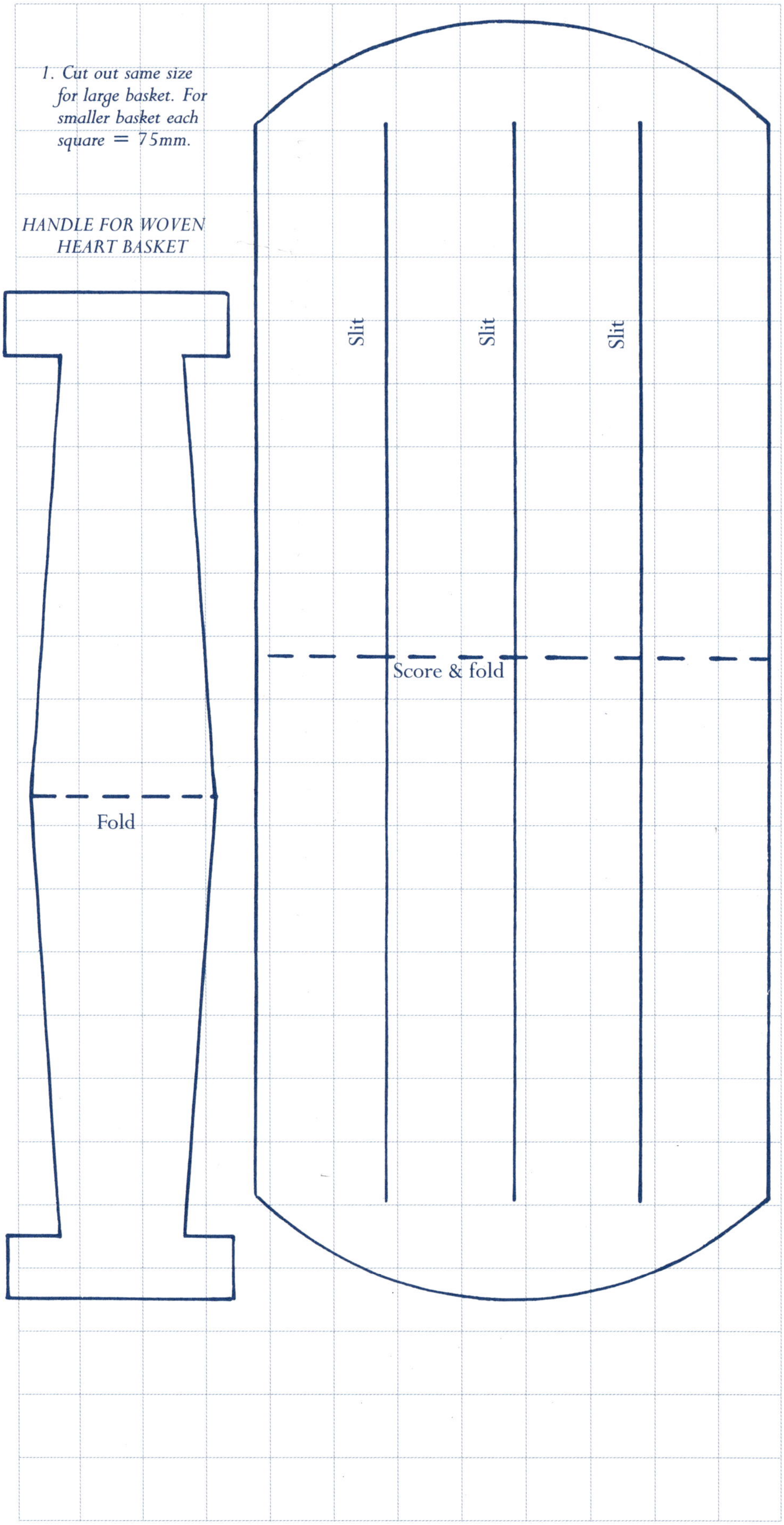

1. *Enlarge by increasing size of each square to 11mm.*

1. *Enlarge and reduce pattern to sizes required.*
2. *Cut out using a scalpel.*
3. *Score folds as marked.*
4. *Fold the straight folds and seal underlap with PVA glue. (see next page)*
5. *When the glue is dry, fold in the side flaps and the box will puff up into a pillow shape.*

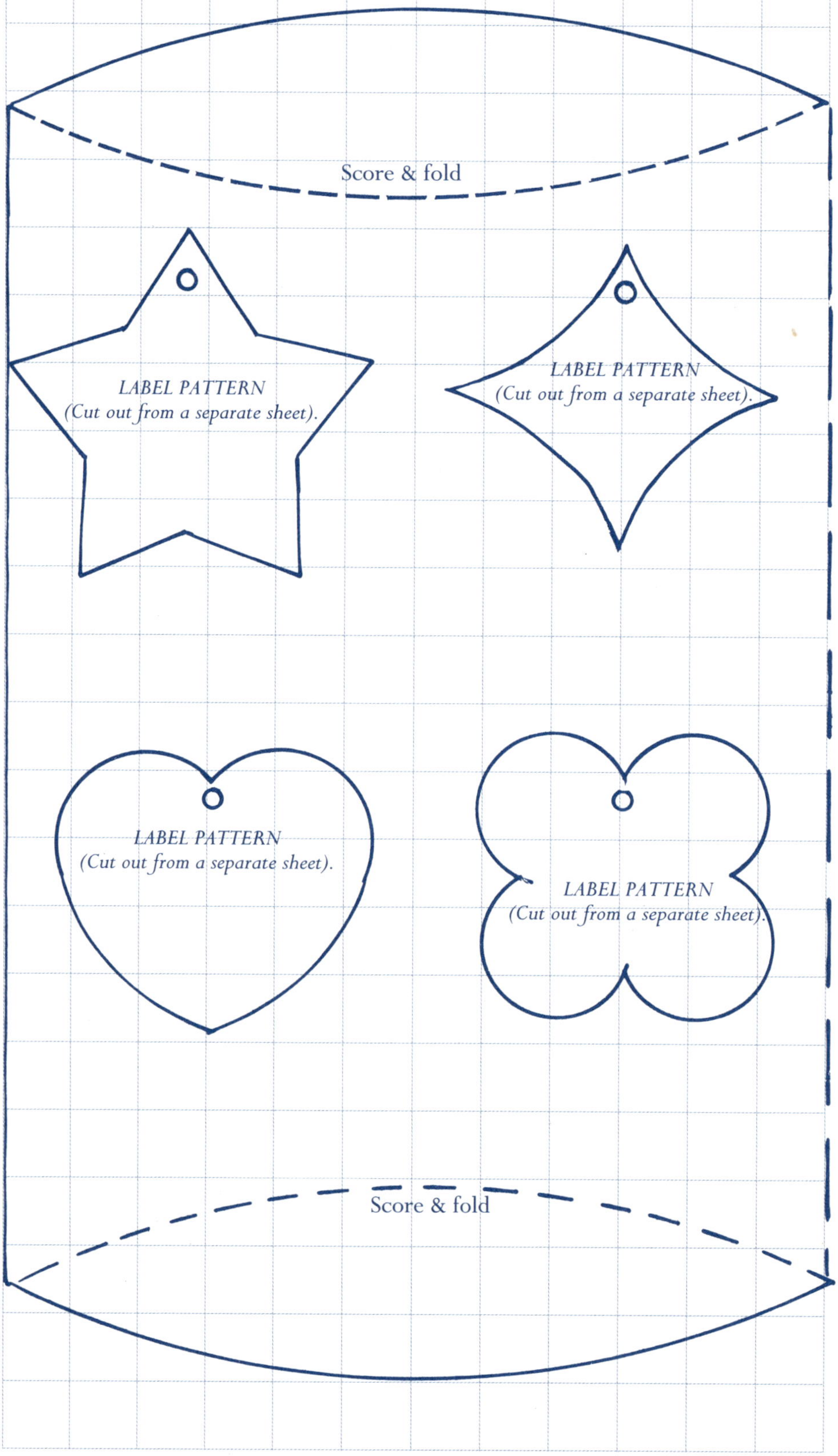

Pattern continues on page 13

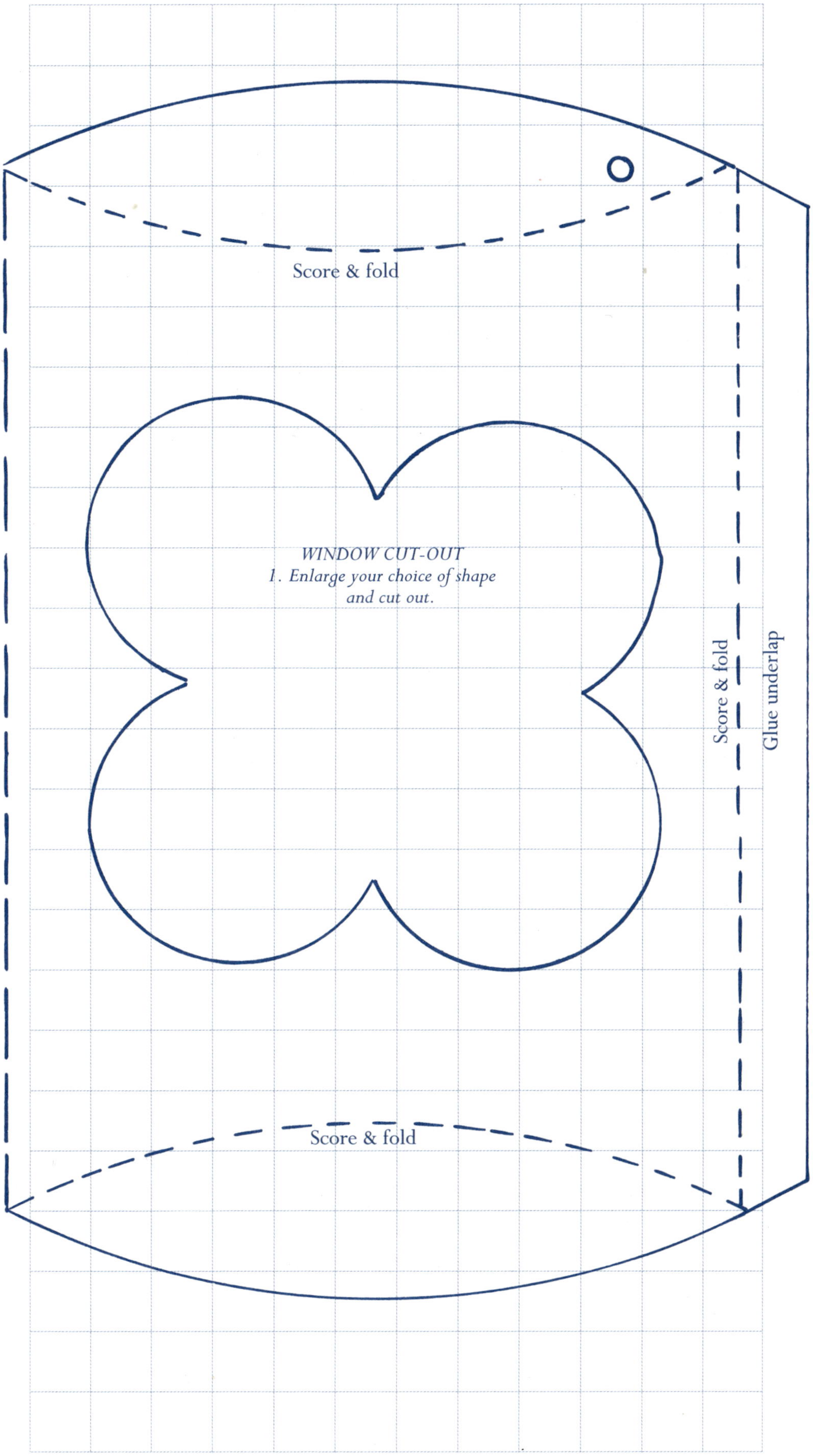

Pattern continued from page 12

BOAT-SHAPED BASKET TEMPLATE

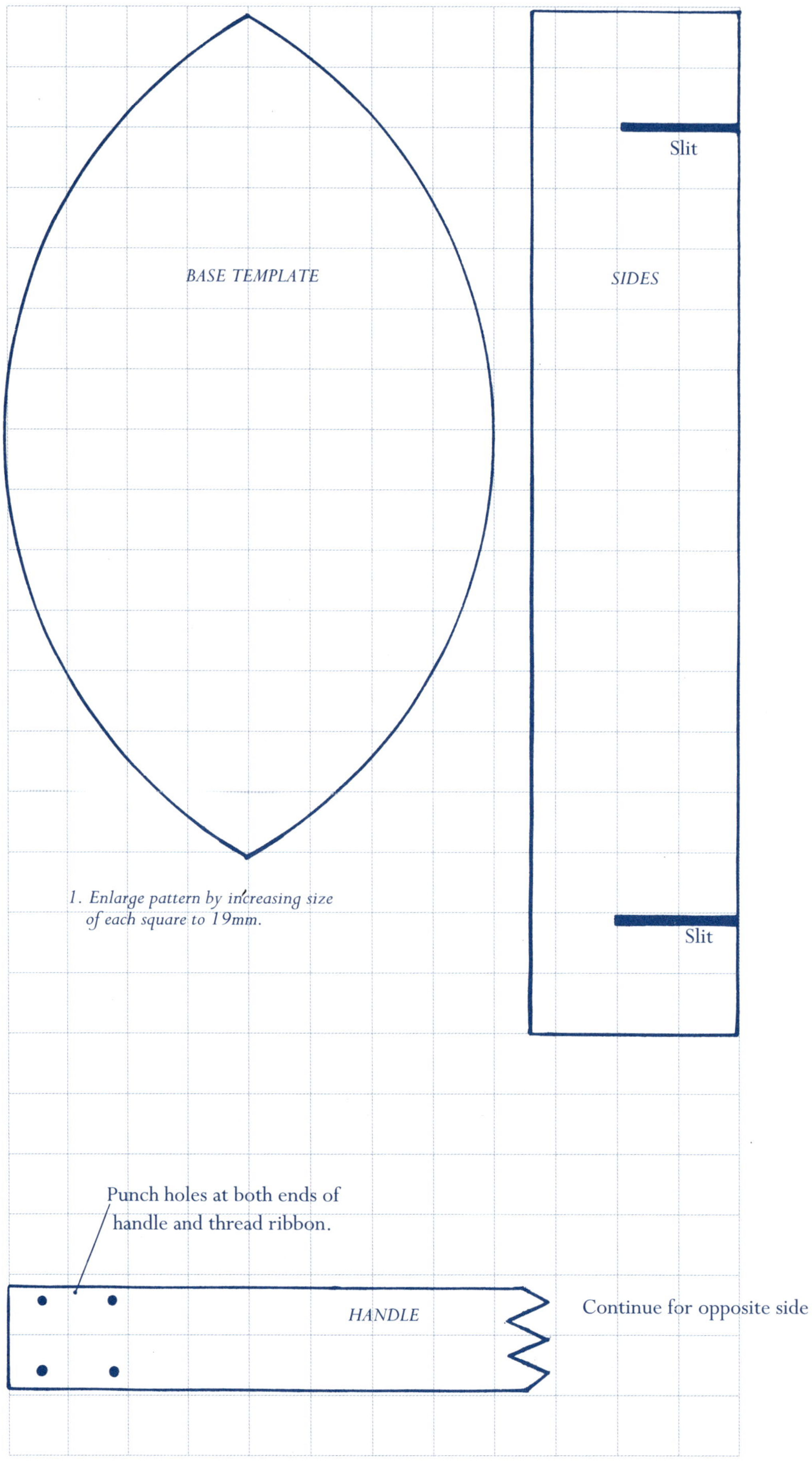

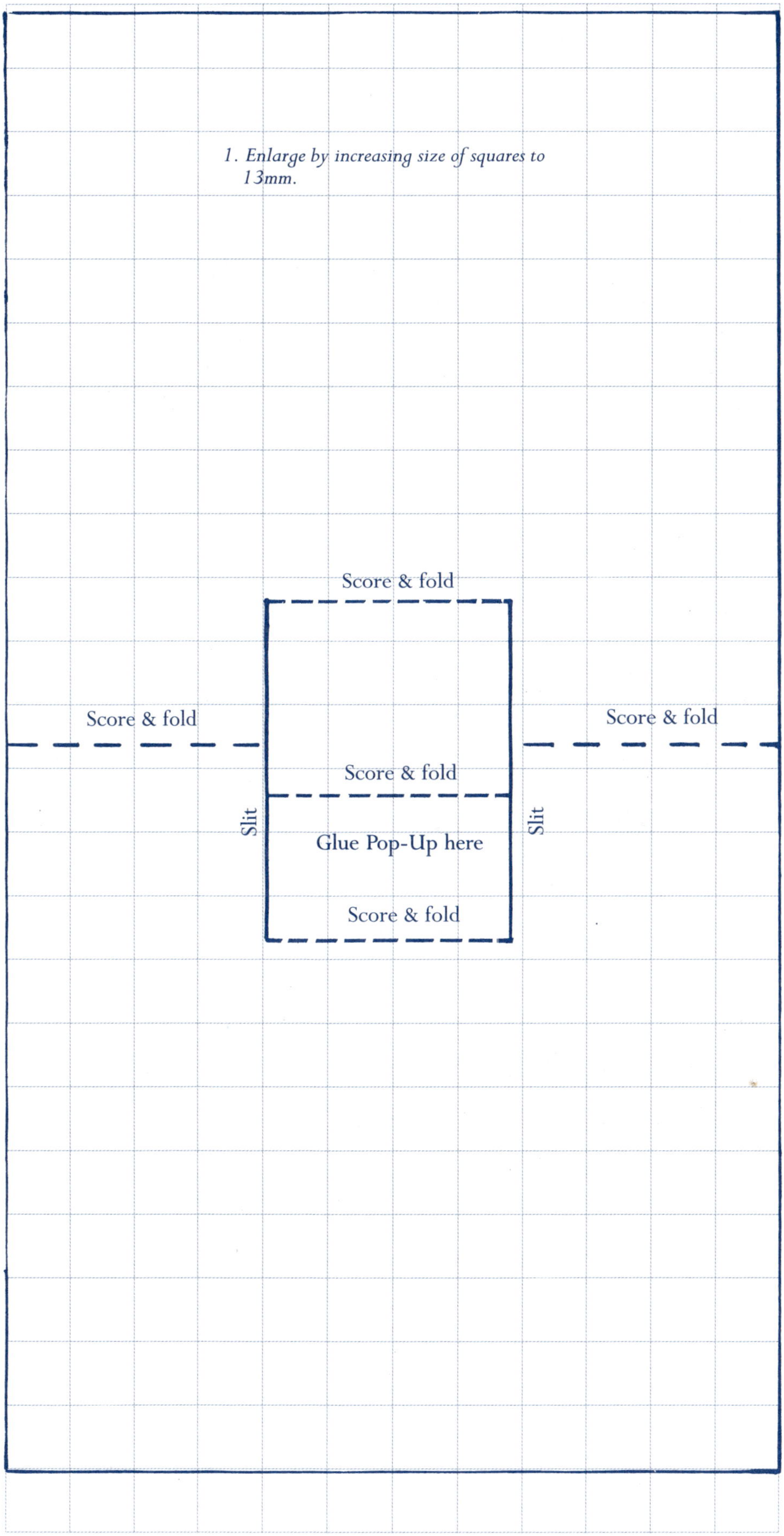
1. Enlarge by increasing size of squares to 13mm.
Score & fold
Score & fold
Score & fold
Score & fold
Slit
Glue Pop-Up here
Slit
Score & fold

1. Enlarge by increasing size of each square to 12mm.
2. Score and fold along marked lines.

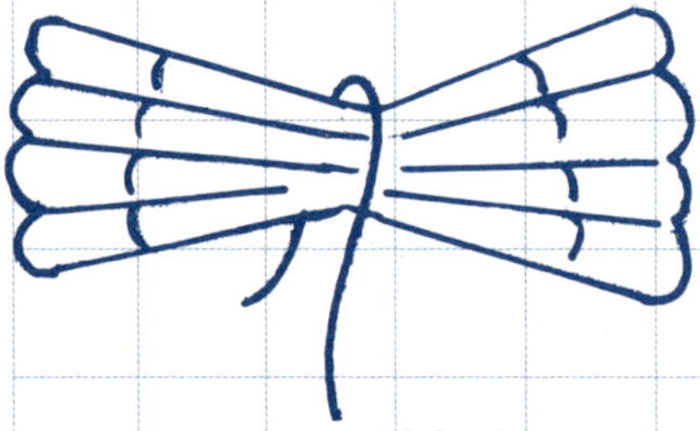

FAN DIAGRAM

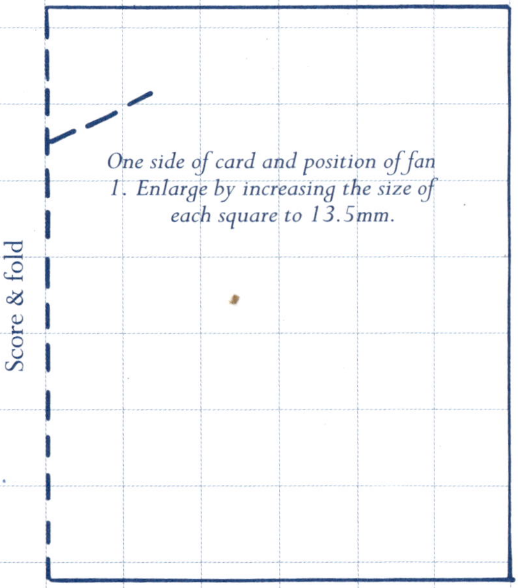
Score & fold
One side of card and position of fan
1. Enlarge by increasing the size of each square to 13.5mm.

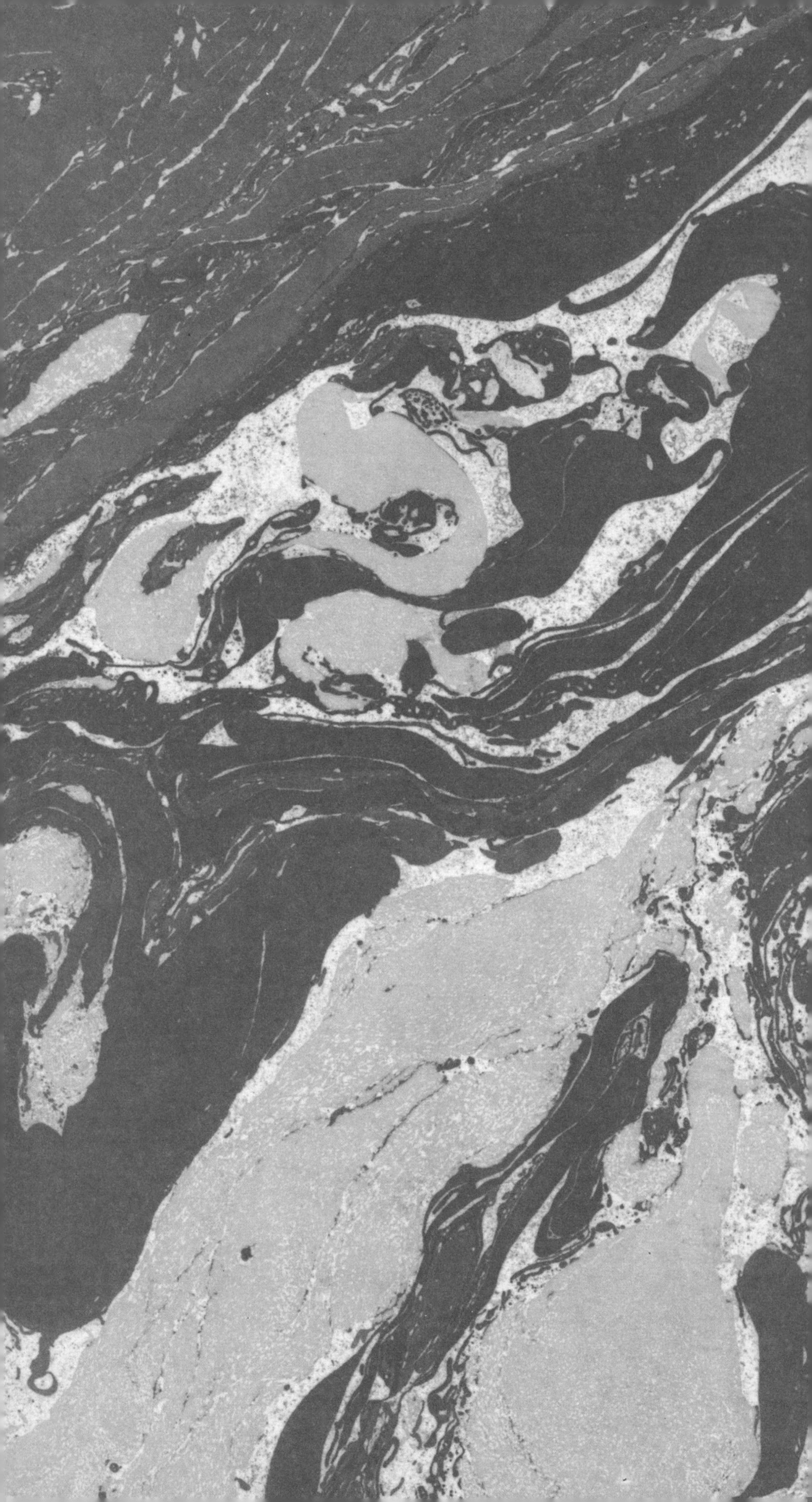